Relational
Database Management
with

ORACLE®

The Practical SQL
    Handbook.
        Emerson, Arnorsky.
    Addison - Wesley.

Relational Database Management with ORACLE®

F.D. Rolland
Manchester Polytechnic

 ADDISON-WESLEY PUBLISHING COMPANY

Wokingham, England · Reading, Massachusetts · Menlo Park, California
New York · Don Mills, Ontario · Amsterdam · Bonn · Sydney
Singapore · Tokyo · Madrid · San Juan

Many of the designations used by manufacturers and sellers to
distinguish their products are claimed as trademarks. Addison-
Wesley has made every attempt to supply trademark information about
manufacturers and their products mentioned in this book. A
list of the trademark designations and their owners appears on
page x.

The programs presented in this book have been included for their
instructional value. They have been tested with care, but are not
guaranteed for any particular purpose. The publisher does not
offer any warranties or representations, nor does it accept any
liabilities with respect to the programs.

Cover designed by Hybert Design & Type, Maidenhead and
printed by The Riverside Printing Co. (Reading) Ltd.
Typeset by Dataset Marlborough Design Ltd, Oxford.
Printed in Great Britain by T.J. Press (Padstow), Cornwall.

First printed 1989

British Library Cataloguing in Publication Data
Rolland, F. D.
    Relational database management with Oracle.
    1. Relational databases. Management. Applications of computer
    systems. Operating systems
    I. Title
    005.75'6

    ISBN 0–201–41647–6

Library of Congress Cataloging in Publication Data available

Preface

At the time of writing, there are a host of companies marketing what they call 'relational' database management systems. This term, the meaning of which is examined in Chapter 1 of the following text, appears to have become compulsory for any newly developed system. There are good reasons why databases should be built on relational principles. The problem is that there are many so-called 'relational' systems that are not, in fact, relational in any meaningful sense. Moreover, relational theory in itself only provides a *framework* for the development of database systems. The theoretical model does not address aspects such as speed of performance or usability of a given system.

Most observers of the software industry agree that there will, in time, be a 'shake-out' in the relational market-place, with many current suppliers falling by the wayside. Of the current suppliers of genuinely relational systems, the Oracle Corporation must be considered one of the best prospects for long-term survival.

Oracle are the longest-established of the independent companies supplying relational systems. They were the first company anywhere to produce a commercially successful relational database management system. Every available market survey indicates that they have continued since that day to lead the field in terms of market penetration and product maturity.

The Oracle DBMS is available on an exceptionally wide range of machines and operating systems, including all of the major computing environments (IBM MVS, DEC VMS, Unix, MS-DOS etc.). It comes in multi-user, single-user, stand-alone, network and distributed modes. In addition to its relational core, Oracle software provides an exceptionally wide range of tools to aid the development and maintenance of complete information systems. This range of tools on top of a relational core has led the Oracle Corporation to claim that they provide a 'fourth generation environment' for the development of computer-based information systems. By this, they mean that their range of products enables the controlled development of computer-based information systems at a speed and with a degree of reliability and user involvement that is simply not feasible with more traditional methodologies.

It is not the role of this text to support or dispute this marketing claim. However, there are examples at the end showing that simple information systems can certainly be built very rapidly using just a few of the Oracle tools. What this book aims to do is to provide an introduction to what is undoubtedly an important and well-established product in the relational market-place.

The introductory chapters describe, in as simple terms as possible, the major aspects of the relational model and just how closely the Oracle system conforms to these. Included is a chapter on the internal architecture of an Oracle system and how closely it adheres to the internationally recommended 3-layer model for database systems. These introductory chapters are followed by an examination of how three of the Oracle tools (SQL*Plus, SQL*Forms and SQL*Report) can be of use in developing a simple information system. These have been chosen as they are the best established of all the Oracle tools. They can be said to represent the 'heart' of any Oracle system and are the only tools at the time of writing that are available on every machine that is capable of running Oracle software. There is also a chapter on database administration which, it is hoped, will be of help to those charged with the management of a multi-user Oracle system.

The purpose of this text is to provide a description and explanation of the major aspects of the Oracle DBMS. Prior detailed knowledge of database management systems is not assumed, though any familiarity with the workings and principles of a computer-based information system will obviously be of help. The text is based on Version 5 of the Oracle software in multi-user mode and is 'inspired' by the author's own experience of running a multi-user Oracle system and teaching others about its use. The Oracle system is genuinely compatible between its many versions and modes of use and the vast majority of this text is directly applicable in the vast majority of Oracle implementations. Any instances where this is not so are carefully indicated.

F.D. Rolland,
Buxton,
1989.

Contents

PART ONE
Oracle as a Relational System

One
The Relational Approach to Database Management

The Oracle Corporation describes its software product as a 'relational' system. This chapter aims to provide an insight into what this should mean, and whether Oracle's product really is 'relational'. This will involve outlining some of theoretical principles underlying modern database management systems, especially those on which the Oracle system is built. These principles are useful in understanding the use of the product. Those readers who are already familiar with the basic concepts underlying relational database systems may wish to go straight to Section 1.3. Those who are not yet familiar with these concepts are strongly advised to read the first two sections, as reference will be made throughout the book to the ideas described therein.

1.1 Why 'relational' databases?

From their earliest days, computers have been used to store files of information. The advantages of computer-based file storage were obvious to the first implementors of electronic information systems. Huge amounts of data could be stored efficiently on magnetic media

3

taking up far less space than the traditional filing cabinet and processed at previously undreamt of speeds. The 1950s and 1960s witnessed an explosive growth in the use of computer-stored data as major corporations throughout the world implemented large-scale electronic data processing systems.

The traditional approach to designing such systems was essentially *ad hoc*. An application would be defined, a file or set of files would be created to support that application and programs written to process the data held on these files. As extensions to the original application definition were identified, further files and programs would be created and written to support them. It soon became clear that this sort of approach had several major defects:

- *Redundancy.*   Many files would end up containing the same data. For instance, an order processing application would be using data that would be common to a number of other applications, such as stock control, customer accounts and so on. The separate development of such applications would mean the re-creation of data in different files, leading to much redundancy of information. In a large corporation, this could mean many million bytes of storage being wastefully used up in duplicating information held elsewhere.

- *Inconsistency.*   The redundancy described above, as well as being wasteful, also gave massive potential for inconsistent data to enter a system. If, for instance, the name of a stock item could appear in a central stock file, in an orders file, in an invoices file, in a customers statements file and so on, the opportunity exists for ascribing many different names to the same item. This leads to confusion and incoherence in a system which can prove very costly.

- *Lack of integration and control.*   This is an inevitable consequence of the above. The replication of the same data across several files in varying formats makes it very difficult, and often impossible, to exercise any effective overall monitoring and control of an information system. For most organizations, the operational data held in their files is the very lifeblood that enables them to function at all, yet an *ad hoc* approach to application development means that this vital resource soon becomes the most uncoordinated and un-organizable entity in the entire business.

As organizations came to realize just how important yet how disorganized their computer-based information systems had become, attention started to focus on a more coherent approach to the *ad hoc* one. In time, this came to be known as the 'database approach'. Broadly speaking, in

(a)

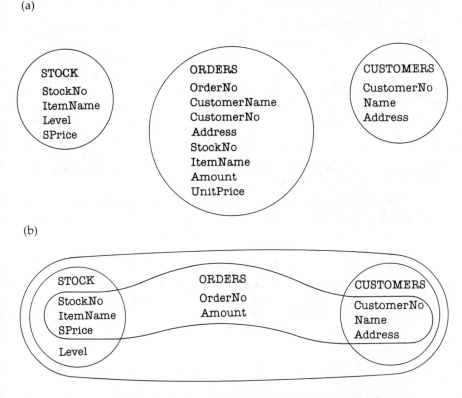

(b)

Figure 1.1 Contrasting the traditional and database approaches to computer file management: (a) the traditional approach: Each application generates its own set of data which may replicate data used by other applications; (b) the database approach: information is a common resource shared by different applications.

this approach, instead of having separate files for separate applications, a firm's data is organized into a single set of underlying files from which the applications draw the data that is relevant to them (see Figure 1.1). In this way, data that is common to a number of applications is only recorded once. When it is updated by one application, it is automatically amended for all other applications that use it. Thus, duplication is eradicated and consistency achieved. Moreover, by having one set of files only, integration of the data between different applications is automatic and central control becomes achievable.

Over the last twenty years, a number of alternative approaches to implementing database management systems have emerged. For large databases, the most widely used ones have been the *hierarchic*, the *network* and the *relational*. The differences between these three approaches to a common problem will now be briefly examined.

1.1.1   Hierarchic databases

In 1968, IBM introduced its customers to its Information Management System (IMS). This was an early attempt to achieve at least some of the aims of the database approach to file management and is one of the earliest examples of a *database management system* (DBMS). In IMS, an organization's data content is viewed hierarchically. Sets of records are related to each other by means of one set of records owning another. For instance, a customer would own a set of orders, an order would own a set of stock items and so on. A record type may only appear at one position in the hierarchy, meaning that if we say an order may own a set of stock items, a stock item cannot own a set of orders. This way, the data is physically organized on a strict hierarchical basis (Figure 1.2).

Hierarchic databases are well suited to those information systems that can be based naturally on the hierarchical model, and there are a

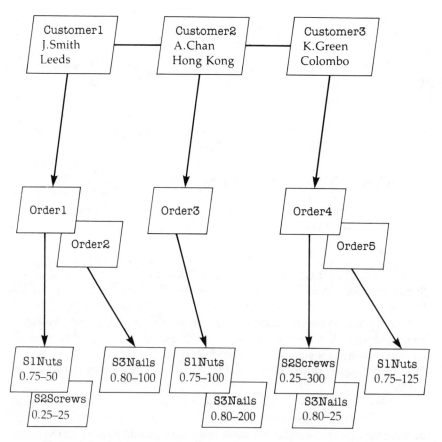

Figure 1.2   A hierarchical representation of some customer/stock/order records.

number of high performance large-scale systems in use that have been built using IMS. However, most systems cannot be implemented in a simple manner in IMS without a dangerously wasteful level of duplication of data. In Figure 1.2, the same stock information is replicated across a number of orders. Moreover, there is no information regarding items for which there are no orders. Thus, there is both duplication and loss of data. This can be overcome in IMS by creating another database for stock alone and setting up a series of elaborate links between the stock and customers' databases. The details of this are complex and out of the scope of this text. However, it is sufficient to say that for most users, hierarchic systems simply do not provide the flexibility and ease of integration that they would expect from the database approach.

1.1.2   Network databases

In the 1970s, the Conference On Data Systems Languages (CODASYL) set up a Database Task Group specifically to produce a set of guidelines for realizing the database approach to file management. What this group produced was a report which was essentially a modification of the hierarchic model. This new model has become known as the CODASYL or network model.

   In the network model, any record may own a set of any other type of record, regardless of whether that other record already owns it. Thus, in our sample database, a customer can own a set of orders, an order can own a set of quantities, each of which are in turn owned by a stock item. Thus, each stock item owns the set of order quantities placed against it. Ownerships between one set of records and another are set up by means of pointers linking a record from one file to a set of records that it owns in another (see Figure 1.3).

   With the network approach, careful data analysis removes redundancies and the files within a system become truly integrated. However, this integration is achieved at the cost of complexity. Network databases are characterized by large numbers of sets of records, each containing a small amount of information and a large number of pointers to other sets of records. Writing even straightforward queries can involve an intricate navigation of the database from one record set to another. For instance, in our sample database, to find the names of the items ordered by customer 1 involves following a path from that customer's record to the first order in the set of orders belonging to that customer. From there, the path goes to the record in the stock file that owns that amount. Having retrieved the name of the item, we then have to step back to the next amount on the order and find its stock owner and so on until there are no more amounts on the order. We then have to step back to the order record that owns these amounts and then find

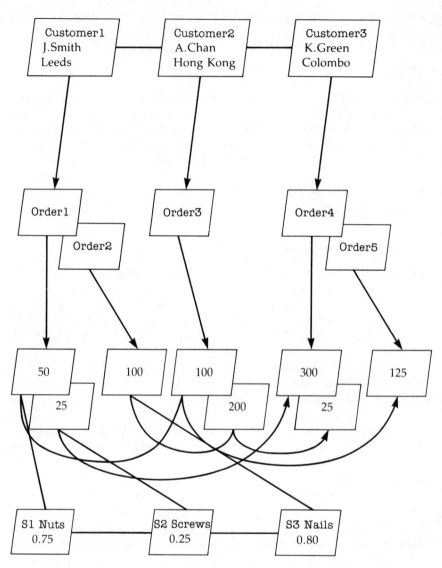

Figure 1.3   A network representation of customers/orders/stock.

the next order owned by that customer and repeat all of the above until there are no more orders for that customer. The programming of all this in the various systems is notoriously complex and error-prone. There are many large network databases in use that do provide efficient data storage and more flexible data structures than those provided by the hierarchical approach. However, these structures are complex and fragmented and thus difficult to use.

1.1.3 Relational databases

In 1970, Dr E.F. Codd, then a research worker for IBM, published a paper: 'A relational model of data for large shared systems', that has since become the single most influential document on database technology. In it, he proposed the 'relational' model for database systems. This model is markedly different to the previously described models and has now become generally accepted as the most coherent and usable model for DBMS development.

In the relational approach, files are treated as two-dimensional tables consisting of rows and columns. Strictly speaking, the tables are called 'relations', the rows 'tuples' and the columns 'attributes'. The tuples are roughly equivalent to what is usually understood to be the records in a file, with the attributes indicating the meanings of the values in each tuple. Thus our sample database would be presented as in Figure 1.4.

There are four relations called Customers, Orders, Stock and OrderLines. The Customers relation has three attributes (CustNo, CustName and Address) and three tuples. The Stock and Orders are similar. The OrderLines table has three attributes, but eight tuples, one for each order against stock. There is some replication of data between the tables, namely those attributes such as CustNo, OrderNo and StockNo which uniquely identify each tuple in their respective relations,

CUSTOMERS

CUSTNO	CUSTNAME	ADDRESS
C1	J. Smith	Leeds
C2	A. Chan	Hong Kong
C3	K. Green	Colombo

ORDERS

ORDERNO	CUSTNO
01	C1
02	C1
03	C2
04	C3
05	C3

STOCK

STOCKNO	SNAME	SPRICE
S1	Nuts	0.75
S2	Screws	0.25
S3	Nails	0.80

ORDERLINES

ORDERNO	STOCKNO	AMOUNT
01	S1	50
01	S2	25
02	S3	100
03	S1	100
03	S3	200
04	S2	300
04	S3	25
05	S1	125

Figure 1.4 A relational representation of customer/orders/stock.

for example, no two Customers tuples hold the same CustNo value. Whereas the network approach uses explicit pointers to link files together, the relational approach enables *relationships* between files to be established on common attribute values. For instance, to find the names of items ordered by Customer 1, the Orders table is searched for all orders with a CustNo value of 1. This will yield a set of order numbers. Then the OrderLines table is searched for all tuples with these order numbers, yielding a set of stock numbers. Lastly the Stock table is searched using this set of stock numbers to find the names of all items ordered by this customer.

Relationships can be established between any two sets of tuples that contain attributes that are built over a common 'domain'. A domain is the pool of allowable values which can be ascribed to an attribute. For example, an attribute which only takes whole numeric values can be said to take the set of integers as its domain and may be used in conjunction with any other attribute that takes the set of integers as its domain to establish a relationship between two sets of tuples. In Figure 1.4 for instance, the CustNo attributes in Orders and Customers are taken from the same domain (the set of allowable customer numbers). Thus a relationship between these two tables can be established on the basis of this common domain.

An important element in the relational model is the concept of *keys*. A key is an attribute or set of attributes which gives each tuple in a relation a unique identity. Thus, CustNo is a key for Customers, StockNo is a key for Stock and OrderNo is a key for Orders. A tuple in OrderLines cannot be identified by its OrderNo or StockNo alone, but the combination of these two attributes will uniquely identify tuples in this relation. Thus, OrderLines has a composite key consisting of two attributes. It is possible for a relation to have more than one key. For instance, a relation could exist representing a file of employees each with a unique works number and a unique National Insurance number. In such a case, these keys are called *candidate keys* and one of them is designated the *primary key* for that relation. In the sample data used in this chapter, each relation in fact only has one candidate key which is, by default, the primary key. A *foreign key* is an attribute in one table that acts as a primary key for another table. For instance, in Orders, CustNo is a foreign key and in OrderLines, OrderNo and StockNo are both individually foreign keys. In a properly analysed relational database, the only data that is replicated between tables are these foreign key attributes, over which the majority of relationsips between relations are established. These provide a far simpler and more flexible method of integrating data from different files than that provided by the network model without the massive scope for redundancy offered by the hierarchical model.

Relational systems provide a development environment that is significantly easier to use than that provided by the other approaches. The data structures are simple to build and easy to understand and writing programs to manipulate them is relatively straightforward. For these reasons, the vast majority of new database systems are based, to a greater or lesser extent, on the relational model. One of the main distinctions of the Oracle DBMS is that it was the first major software product to appear on the market based directly on the relational model and is without doubt the most mature of all the currently available relational products.

1.2   How relational is the Oracle DBMS?

The relational approach to data management differs to that of the network or the hierarchical approaches in that it is based on precise mathematical principles. Thus, it is theoretically possible to measure precisely how relational a given DBMS is. This is useful because there are a number of products currently on the market that claim to be relational but which, in fact, support little or none of Codd's original model. There is, at the time of writing, no product that completely satisfies the relational model as defined by Date (1986, 1987, 1988). However, there are a number of products, including the Oracle system, that satisfy the most important features of the relational model.

According to Date, there are three main parts to the relational model:

- Data structures,
- Data manipulation,
- Data integrity.

A brief discussion of these follows.

1.2.1   Relational data structures

As mentioned above, a relational database deals with files that are presented as two-dimensional tables consisting of rows and columns. The columns of a table are called its *attributes* and the rows its *tuples*. One important property of these tables (or relations) is that at any row/column intersection, the values that are found are *atomic* – they are not sets of values which may be sub-divided into subsets. For example, with our OrderLines relation, the following representation in Figure 1.5 would break the atomicity rule. Instead, the relational model requires a representation such as indicated in Figure 1.4, where each 'cell' in each relation contains *one, and only one*, value. For example, for each Stock

Order No.	Stocknos	Amounts
1	{1,2}	{50,25}
2	{3}	{100}
3	{1,3}	{100,200}
4	{1,2}	{300,25}
5	{1}	{125}

Figure 1.5   A representation for the OrderLines file using set values.

tuple, there is just one StockNo, one SName and one Amount, and so on. Atomicity is important as it enables a small but powerful set of operators to be defined for relational systems that satisfy all the standard data retrieval requirements of a DBMS.

In terms of its basic data structures, the Oracle DBMS satisfies the relational definition.

1.2.2   Relational data manipulation

Any DBMS requires a set of data manipulation operations to extract data from the system. A relational system requires only eight types of operation to effect all possible combinations of data extraction. All relational data manipulation operations take a set of tuples derived from one or more relations as their domain and map these to a new set of tuples that, in themselves, constitute a relation. In the following illustrations, a very simple notation will be used to describe each of these operations. The notation is a form of what is commonly referred to as *relational algebra*. This is not to be confused with the language used to create and use the Oracle software (SQL) which superficially bears some resemblance to the relational algebra in its notation, it is, in fact, a quite different sort of language in certain fundamental respects.

Date identifies eight basic relational operations. Five of these (SELECT, PROJECT, UNION, MINUS and TIMES) are primitives and the other three (JOIN, INTERSECT and DIVIDE) may be constructed from the primitives, but are distinct enough to merit separate description.

1.2.2.1   *The* SELECT *operation*
The SELECT operation extracts specified tuples from a relation. For example, using our OrderLines relation in Figure 1.4, a Select can be implemented to find all the orders placed for a particular item:

    Select OrderLines where StockNo = 3

will yield

OrderNo	StockNo	Amount
2	3	100
3	3	200
4	3	25

1.2.2.2   *The* PROJECT *operation*

PROJECT will extract all the values for an attribute or set of attributes in a relation with resulting duplicate tuples being removed if necessary. For example:

Project OrderLines (StockNo)

will yield

StockNo
1
2
3

representing the set of values ascribed to StockNo in the OrderLines relation.

A Project may be implemented over more than one attribute at a time. For instance:

Project OrderLines (OrderNo, StockNo)

will yield the output shown in Table 1.1

Table 1.1   PROJECT on two attributes.

OrderNo	StockNo
1	1
1	2
2	3
3	1
3	3
4	2
4	3
5	1

Table 1.2   The JOIN operation on Orders and OrderLines.

OrderNo	CustNo	StockNo	Amount
1	1	1	50
1	1	2	25
2	1	3	100
3	2	1	100
3	2	3	200
4	3	2	300
4	3	3	25
5	3	1	125

1.2.2.3   *The* JOIN *operation*

JOIN is used to combine relations together. The simplest type of JOIN is the equijoin whereby two relations are joined on the basis of an attribute being common to both relations containing equal values. For instance, to combine the Orders information with the OrderLines information, we can use the OrderNo attribute common to both tables:

Join Orders, OrderLines (OrderNo)

to yield the output shown in Table 1.2

This operation has taken all the tuples from the Orders relation and joined them with all those tuples in the OrderLines relation that have the same OrderNo value.

Of course, further JOINs can be implemented in order to combine names and addresses of Customers from the Customers table and names and prices of Stock items from the Stock table into the output above.

1.2.2.4   *The* UNION *operator*

The UNION of two relations is the set of tuples that belong to either or both of two compatible relations. Suppose the Customers relation was partitioned into four separate relations according to customer address, resulting in a set of NorthWest, SouthWest, NorthEast, and SouthEast relations. NorthWest UNION NorthEast would give a composite relation consisting of all customers residing in the north.

1.2.2.5   *The* INTERSECT *operation*

The INTERSECT operation on two compatible sets of tuples yields those tuples that belong to both sets. For instance, NorthWest INTERSECT NorthEast would yield all those customers who had, for some reason, been placed in both of these regions.

Table 1.3 Stock TIMES Customers.

StockNo	Sname	SPrice	Custno	Custname	Address
1	Nuts	0.75	1	J. Smith	Leeds
2	Screws	0.25	1	J. Smith	Leeds
3	Nails	0.80	1	J. Smith	Leeds
1	Nuts	0.75	2	A. Chan	Hong Kong
2	Screws	0.25	2	A. Chan	Hong Kong
3	Nails	0.80	2	A. Chan	Hong Kong
1	Nuts	0.75	3	K. Green	Colombo
2	Screws	0.25	3	K. Green	Colombo
3	Nails	0.80	3	K. Green	Colombo

1.2.2.6   The MINUS *operation*

When applied to two compatible sets of tuples, the MINUS operation yields all those tuples that belong to the first set, but not to the second. NorthWest MINUS NorthEast yields those customers who have been classified in the North-West and not in the North-East as well.

It is perfectly possible to build INTERSECTions purely from applying the appropriate UNION and MINUS operations to two given relations. However, it is more convenient and natural to regard INTERSECT as a separate operation.

1.2.2.7   The TIMES *operation*

This operation yields the Cartesian product of two relations. For instance, using the relations in Figure 1.4, Stock TIMES Customers would yield a relation consisting of all the Customer tuples paired off with all the stock tuples, as shown in Table 1.3. The JOIN operation is in fact a special, restricted, form of the TIMES operation.

1.2.2.8   The DIVIDE *operation*

The DIVIDE operation is most easily illustrated by using two relations, one consisting of two attributes and the other consisting of one. If we have two relations **A** and **B** containing the data given in Table 1.4, then A DIVIDE B would yield

Cno

3
5

Table 1.4   A simple DIVIDE.

A		B
CustNo	StockNo	StockNo
1	1	1
1	2	2
2	2	3
3	1	
3	3	
3	2	
4	2	
4	3	
5	3	
5	2	
5	1	

This is because, in relation A, those tuples with a Cno 3 or 5 have next to them all the Sno values (1, 2 and 3) in relation B. The DIVIDE operation when applied to two relations whose attributes overlap returns the non-overlapping attribute values for all those tuples in the first relation that match all the tuples in the second.

The DIVIDE operation can be built using PROJECT, SELECT, MINUS and JOIN operations. Once again, though, it is more convenient and natural to think of it as a separate operation.

According to Date, to be relationally complete, a DBMS must support the afore-mentionned data structures and provide the full functionality of the eight relational operations. By this definition, therefore, the Oracle system is relationally complete.

1.2.3   Relational data integrity

Although the Oracle DBMS is relationally complete, it is not fully relational. To be fully relational, a product must be relationally complete, allow domain definition *and* provide *entity integrity* and *referential integrity*.

As explained in Section 1.1, the values that an attribute may take are drawn from what is called its domain. In common with most products, Oracle provides a number of predefined domains such as *integer, number, character, real* and *date*. There are, however, no facilities for the system user to define their own domains.

Entity integrity is based on the use of primary keys for uniquely identifying tuples. A primary key may be composed of one or more attributes for a given relation. Entity integrity requires that for any attribute that participates in a primary key for a relation, no tuple may take on a null value for that attribute. In other words, if the primary key for the Customers relation is CustNo, every tuple in that relation must have a CustNo value. The key used for OrderLines is of necessity a composite one, consisting of OrderNo and StockNo. This means that every tuple in that relation must have an OrderNo value and a StockNo value to satisfy entity integrity. Entity integrity ensures that no relation may contain duplicate tuples.

Referential integrity concerns foreign keys: those attributes in a relation that act as a primary key into another relation. In our OrderLines relation, StockNo is a foreign key to Stock, and OrderNo is a foreign key to Orders. Referential integrity requires that for any attribute or set of attributes in a relation that comprise a foreign key, the values assigned to these attributes must also exist in the relation for which they are the primary key. For example, in the OrderLines relation, it would not be allowed by referential integrity for OrderNo values to be inserted that did not exist in the Orders relation or StockNo values that did not exist in the Stock relation. Furthermore, referential integrity would restrict actions such as deleting Customers from the Customers relation if there are Orders in the Orders relation containing their CustNo value.

The Oracle software uses Structured Query Language (SQL) for defining and manipulating relations. SQL has no direct mechanism for defining or recognizing a key. It is possible to fabricate entity integrity by requiring that certain attributes in a relation are not allowed to take on null values. However, these do not have to be primary key attributes and it is not compulsory to do this. It is also possible to define a relation that can take on null values for any or all of its attributes. Thus, a form of entity integrity is achievable, but only indirectly, and it is not compulsory. It is therefore possible to build relations in the Oracle system which have duplicate tuples, which entity integrity is designed to disallow. Relations that contain duplicate tuples are not strictly relations at all, but simply tables of atomic values. For this reason, in later chapters, this text will refer to Oracle data structures as 'tables' rather than 'relations' as they are not relations in the true sense. In a similar fashion, referential integrity may be fabricated indirectly in the Oracle system, but is not compulsory for any given set of relations. Thus, it is possible to reference tuples from one relation to the next that do not actually exist.

As the Oracle DBMS does not provide domain definition and because it does not *automatically* enforce referential and entity integrity for all relations, it cannot be described as *fully relational*. There are, in fact, no products on the market that are truly fully relational. The Oracle system is relationally complete, meaning that it provides the basic data structures and operations required by the relational model. The integrity rules are also highly desirable, but not *essential*. Many thousands of relationally complete systems have been installed worldwide, a high proportion of them supplied by the Oracle Corporation. To implement the integrity rules would require significant extensions to the software without necessarily giving a corresponding increase in its functionality. The Oracle Corporation have instead concentrated on providing a relationally complete system backed up by a wide range of software tools aimed at enhancing its functionality for the data user. The Oracle system aims to be more than a database management system. Its main purpose is to provide an environment for the development of computer-based information systems built on top of the relational model.

1.3   Oracle's extensions to the relational model

> The fact that a given system is relational . . . does not in itself guarantee that the system in question is a 'good system'.
>
> *C.J. Date* (1986)

The relational model addresses issues such as data structures and the query operations to be performed on them. It says nothing about important factors such as the user interface, the ease of processing of the data, the required performance of the system and so on. The Oracle DBMS provides a significant number of enhancements to the relational model, possibly more than any other currently available product. This does not necessarily mean that it is the *best* of all the relational products. The comparative quality of the many different relational systems available is a controversial topic which is outside the scope of this text. What is irrefutable is the fact that the Oracle Corporation currently has the most widespread market penetration of all relationally based systems, having made significant inroads into the mainframe, mini- and microcomputer markets. The Oracle DBMS is the most mature of all these products and arguably provides the most comprehensive set of software tools. In addition to the relational kernel, the Oracle Corporation supply the following components:

1. *SQL*Plus*   SQL is the *de facto* industry standard language for building and querying relational databases. When using SQL in an interactive mode, Oracle users have at their disposal a number of extra commands which can further process and format the output from an SQL command, as well as providing facilities for editing and saving SQL command files. Oracle call this extended programming interface *SQL*Plus*.

2. *SQL*Forms*   Most users of a database will not be programmers. The *SQL*Forms* package allows the creation of form-based applications for the manipulation and querying of a database through customized screens.

3. *SQL*Report*   This module allows formatting, specification and generation of complex reports combining text with data derived and processed from an Oracle system.

4. *SQL*Menu*   This allows menu-driven applications to be built which can call up reports, forms and programs generated in other modules.

5. *Easy*SQL*   This is an interface to Oracle that by means of pull-down menus and windows seeks to minimize the amount of keyboard use and programming knowledge that a user requires to develop Oracle applications.

6. *SQL*Calc* and *SQL*Graph*   These two modules provide spreadsheet and graphics interfaces to the Oracle system. They are marketed as decision support tools.

7. *CASE* (Computer aided systems engineering)   This module is intended to provide support for the designers and implementors of computer-based information systems. By means of a series of forms and graphical interfaces, designers can record and model the assumptions and decisions made about a system which are then cross-referenced and checked against previous design decisions to ensure system compatibility and design integrity. A system dictionary is built and a default database and associated documentation based on the contents of the dictionary may be generated. The aim is to provide a controlled environment for the design, implementation and maintenance of complete systems.

Further descriptions of the above products are given in Appendix IV: Oracle Products Summary.

In the next chapter, the underlying physical organization of an Oracle database will be described prior to consideration of the most central of the user tools listed above (*SQL*Plus*, *SQL*Forms* and *SQL*Report*).

Key points

● An unstructured approach to file management on computers can easily lead to data that contains large-scale redundancies and inconsistencies.

- The database approach provides an organization with the means to achieving centralized and integrated control over its data as well as the mechanism for reducing inconsistency and redundancy.

- Of the major approaches to database modelling, the relational method is the only one which combines flexibility with simplicity.

- The relational model is based on mathematical principles. As such, it is possible to measure how *relational* a product is.

- The Oracle DBMS can be regarded as a relationally complete product. This means that it provides the data structures and operations required by the relational model.

- The Oracle Corporation supply a number of software tools that run on top of its relational kernel that collectively comprise a 'Fourth Generation' environment for software development.

EXERCISES

1.1   Explain what is meant by the term *database*.

1.2   List and describe the disadvantages of a non-database approach to computer file management.

1.3   Draw a table with three columns with the headings *Hierarchic, Network* and *Relational*. Under each column, list the advantages and disadvantages of each of these approaches to database management.

1.4   Define the following terms:
(a)   relation,
(b)   tuple,
(c)   attribute,
(d)   relationship,
(e)   candidate key,
(f)   primary key,
(g)   foreign key.

1.5   What would be the output from the following algabraic operations on the database in Figure 1.4:
(a)   SELECT Customers where Address = 'Leeds',
(b)   PROJECT Stock (Sname),
(c)   JOIN Stock, Orders (Stockno)?

1.6   Specify the algabraic operations necessary to:
(a)   Find the Stock record with an Sname of 'Nuts',
(b)   Generate a list of Customer names,

(c) Append the name and address of the Customer who has placed a particular order to each order record in the Orders relation.

1.7 What are the differences between database systems that are:
(a) minimally relational,
(b) relationally complete,
(c) fully relational?

References

E.F. Codd (1970). A relational model of data for large shared data banks. *Comm ACM*, **13**, (6).

C.J. Date (1986). *An Introduction to Database Systems* Vol 1. Reading, MA: Addison-Wesley.

C.J. Date (1987). *A Guide to Ingres*. Reading, MA: Addison-Wesley.

C.J.Date and C.J. White (1988). *A Guide to DB2* 2nd. Edn. Reading, MA: Addison-Wesley.

Two
The Oracle Database Architecture

As we have seen, the user of a relational type database system such as the Oracle DBMS perceives the data as being stored in a series of tables. These tables comprise a *logical* view of data that is held in physical files written to and retrieved from disk by the underlying computer's operating system. The details of how computers actually represent, store and retrieve data from disk vary from one operating system to another and are ultimately governed by the physical characteristics of the underlying computer hardware. Any database management system, be it hierarchical, network or relational, requires a software interface that 'maps' the physically stored data to the logical user view.

ANSI/SPARC (1978) published a report that set out a standard approach to representing this interface. Since this report was published, it has become the usual practice to consider a database management system to be comprised of three layers: the *external*, the *internal* and the *conceptual*.

- The *external layer* is the set of views that the users of a database have of a system. It consists of the logical structure of the files that are available to them, and the rights and permissions that they have. In a multi-user system, there will be a number of external views of the datafiles, each effectively comprising a subset of the total information content of the database.

- The *internal layer* provides the interface between the file structures peculiar to the database and the file structures that are used by the host computer's operating system. The role of this layer is to organize the files in such a way that they can be handled by the underlying operating system. The actual storage and retrieval of the files remains under the control of the operating system.

- The *conceptual layer* represents the interface between the external and internal layers. It is a logical representation of the entire information content of the database.

The purpose of this layering scheme is to ease the maintainability of a system. If users' views were mapped directly to disk, then every change in the physical storage of the database would necessitate the mapping of every user's view to be re-written. Instead, the users interact with a logical view of the entire database as represented by the conceptual layer. The conceptual layer is itself underpinned by the internal layer which converts the conceptual file structures which will be peculiar to the given database into general file structures that can be mapped by the operating system to actual stored data on disk. There exists, therefore, one mapping between the conceptual and the internal representations, and one mapping between the internal representation and the operating system (Figure 2.1). General housekeeping routines can be carried out on the disk storage by the operating system that may rearrange the physical data structures held on disk, but these changes are effectively invisible to the user of the DBMS. An upgrade or change to the operating system will ideally mean that all that needs to be modified is the interface between the operating system and the internal layer.

Of course, this is an ideal view that is rarely achieved in its full purity in practice. For performance reasons alone, internal representations of databases tend to be highly tuned for particular operating systems and may even by-pass the operating system altogether. With Oracle running on Unix implementations, for instance, it is possible to set up a database that is mapped directly to a raw disk device, by-passing the Unix file management facilities altogether. However, this mapping is still from an internal representation that underpins a logical view of the whole system. The logical view remains effectively shielded from the physical representation. Relational systems are noted for their ability to conform to the three-layer view of database architectures.

In the following description, the Oracle architecture will be described in its internal and external manifestations.

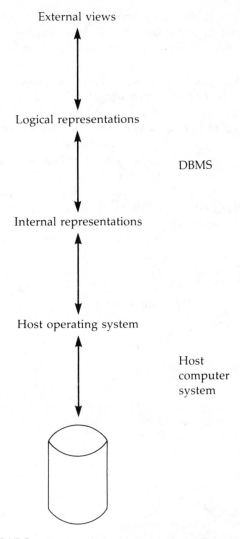

Figure 2.1 ANSI/SPARC-recommended 3-layer model for databases.

2.1 The external view of an Oracle database

To the user community, an Oracle database is comprised of a set of user accounts. Each account has a user name and is protected by a password. According to its privileges and permissions, an account may create, access and update a set of tables. The ability to create tables is determined by an account's basic privileges (see below). An account may access and update the tables that it has created. It may also access and update tables that have been created by other accounts provided those other accounts have explicitly granted it permission to do so. An account may grant similar permissions on its own tables to other accounts (see Section 3.1.4).

There are three types of basic privilege: Connect, Resource and DBA, the latter being an acronym for Database Administrator. Users that have only the Connect privilege may log onto an Oracle database and access and update those tables to which they have been granted the appropriate permissions. They cannot create tables, but may create *views*. A view is a logical table specified by the user which does not actually physically exist, but instead draws its data from one or more stored physical tables. Users with Resource privilege may create their own tables and grant privileges on these tables to other users. Users with DBA status may grant and revoke Connect, Resource and DBA privileges to and from other users, create and alter partitions (see Section 2.2), perform full database exports onto back-up storage and access and update any other user's data. Thus, all accounts are originally created and controlled by the DBA account(s).

All Oracle systems are initially installed with three special user accounts: Sys, System and Public. Sys and System both have DBA privileges. Together, they own the tables and views that comprise the Oracle Data Dictionary. This is a collection of tables and views which acts as a reference guide to the information content of the entire database. DTAB, shown in Table 2.1, acts as a list of contents for the data dictionary.

Table 2.1   The Oracle data dictionary as listed in DTAB.

TABLE	REMARKS
AUDIT_ACCESS	Audit entries for accesses to user's tables/views (DBA sees all)
AUDIT_ACTIONS	Maps auditing action numbers to action names
AUDIT_CONNECT	Audit trail entries for user logon/logoff (DBA sees all users)
AUDIT_DBA	Audit trail entries for DBA activities – for DBA use only
AUDIT_EXISTS	Audit trail entries for objects which do not exist – DBAs only
AUDIT_TRAIL	Audit trail entries relevant to the user (DBA sees all)
CATALOG	Tables and views accessible to user (excluding data dictionary)
CLUSTERS	Clusters and their tables (either must be accessible to user)
CLUSTERCOLUMNS	Maps cluster columns to clustered table columns
COL	Specifications of columns in tables created by the user

TABLE	REMARKS
COLUMNS	Columns in tables accessible to user (excluding data dictionary)
DEFAULT_AUDIT	Default table auditing options
DTAB	Description of tables and views in Oracle's data dictionary
EXTENTS	Data structure of extents within tables
INDEXES	Indexes created by user and indexes on tables created by user
PARTITIONS	File structure of files within partitions – for DBA use only
PRIVATESYN	Private synonyms created by the user
PUBLICSYN	Public synonyms
SESSIONS	Audit trail entries for the user's sessions (DBA sees all)
SPACES	Selection of space definitions for creating tables and clusters
STORAGE	Data and index storage allocation for user's own tables
SYNONYMS	Synonyms, private and public
SYSAUDIT_TRAIL	Synonym for sys.audit_trail – for DBA use only
SYSCATALOG	Profile of tables and views accessible to the user
SYSCOLAUTH	Directory of column update access granted by or to the user
SYSCOLUMNS	Specifications of columns in accessible tables and views
SYSEXTENTS	Data structure of tables throughout system – for DBA use only
SYSINDEXES	List of indexes, underlying columns, creator, and options
SYSPROGS	List of programs precompiled by user
SYSSTORAGE	Summary of all database storage – for DBA use only
SYSTABALLOC	Data and index space allocations for all tables – for DBAs
SYSTABAUTH	Directory of access authorization granted by or to the user
SYSTEM_AUDIT	System auditing options – for DBA use only
SYSUSERAUTH	Master list of Oracle users – for DBA use only
SYSUSERLIST	List of Oracle users
SYSVIEWS	List of accessible views
TAB	List of tables, views, clusters and synonyms created by the user
TABALLOC	Data and index space allocations for all user's tables
TABQUOTAS	Table allocation (space) parameters for tables created by user
TABLE_AUDIT	Auditing options of user's tables and views (DBA sees all)
VIEWS	Defining SQL statements for views created by the user
DBLINKS	Public and private links to external databases
SYSDBLINKS	All links to external databases – for DBA use only

The whole of the data dictionary is visible only to those accounts with DBA status. Views such as SysStorage and Partitions are accessible to DBAs only. Tables such as Audit-Trail and Table-Audit provide information about only those tables accessible to the user. As all tables and views are accessible to DBA users, these also yield system-wide information to DBAs whilst yielding a subset of this information to other users. Tables such as Catalog yield information that is particular to the account from which they are being queried. Catalog, for instance, lists those tables and views that have been created by the user along with the names and owners of other tables and views to which they have been explicitly granted access. Certain other views such as SysUserList and tables such as DTAB provide all users with system-wide information.

The data dictionary thus provides a logical framework for the entire data content of an Oracle system. The names and definitions of all data objects (tables, views, indexes, space definitions, and so on) are recorded here along with the space used by the objects, the names, passwords and privileges of all the accounts and the rights and the permissions that accounts have granted to each other. As such, the dictionary is fundamental to the operation of an Oracle database. Under no circumstance should a user attempt to log onto the Sys or System accounts and attempt to update the tables owned by them. It is the responsibility of the Database Administrator to protect these accounts from unwelcome interference.

The special user Public has the Connect privilege only. Any privileges granted by an account to the user Public are automatically granted to all other user accounts. Thus, if a user has a table that they wish to be available for access to all other users, they can grant this privilege to Public instead of having to list every single user in the system.

2.2   The internal organization of an Oracle database

In Version 5 of the Oracle DBMS, the tables of data that comprise the data content of a given Oracle database reside in a single logical database file (the DB file). The DB file itself consists of one or more partitions which themselves consist of one or more actual files stored on disk (see Figure 2.2).

Partitions are logical units which can only be manipulated from within the Oracle software itself. A user of an Oracle database can see individual partitions, but cannot see from within the system the actual physical files that comprise a partition. All that they see is a collection of tables held within partitions which the DBMS itself maps to underlying physical files. The data in the tables may in fact overlap the boundaries

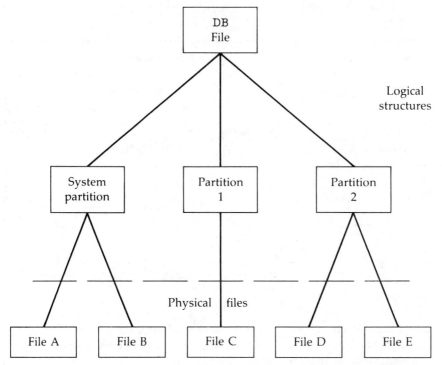

Figure 2.2   The underlying Oracle file structure.

between the physical files. This is, however, invisible to the database user, along with the other physical details of how the data is actually stored.

Each Oracle database starts with a partition named System which contains one physical file. Extra partitions may be created by users with DBA status and, likewise, extra physical files can be added to a partition. All user tables are by default stored in the System partition unless specified otherwise by the user. Apart from users' tables, the System partition also contains the tables that comprise the Oracle Data Dictionary, the help tables providing on-line assistance to users, and the temporary tables that are created when certain Oracle commands are executed.

When a table is first created by a user, a space is automatically assigned for it within a partition (by default the System partition). The Oracle Data Dictionary contains a table called Spaces which holds details of all the space definitions available within a system. Each system has a default space definition, the actual size of which is operating-system dependent. Alternative space definitions may be added to the Data Dictionary (see Section 8.5 below).

To the user, a table consists of rows and columns. At the internal

Row No	Row length
Column ID	Column length
Data	
Column ID	Column length
Data	

Figure 2.3   Overhead information for Oracle data blocks. Row information is repeated for each row stored, column information for each column in a row.

level, the Oracle software requires overhead information for every table and for every row and column that participates in a table – see Figure 2.3.

At the table level, the overhead information includes items such as the start and end address of each block of storage (its *extent*) used by the table, the number of storage blocks in each extent, and data dictionary information such as the type of data held in each column. This latter piece of information saves the system from having to find the data dictionary definition for a table every time data is added to it, even though it does represent a duplication of data already stored within the dictionary.

For each row there is information stored such as its sequence number and its length in bytes. For each column within each row there is stored its identification number and its length in bytes (see Figure 2.4). These overheads are necessary in order for the data to be stored in a suitably compressed format. All that the user sees is the data content of the columns, though they can also access the row sequence numbers if they wish.

2.3   Summary

At the external level, an Oracle database is comprised of a set of tables owned by user accounts. The tables that are visible to and usable by a user depends upon the rights and privileges granted to that user. These

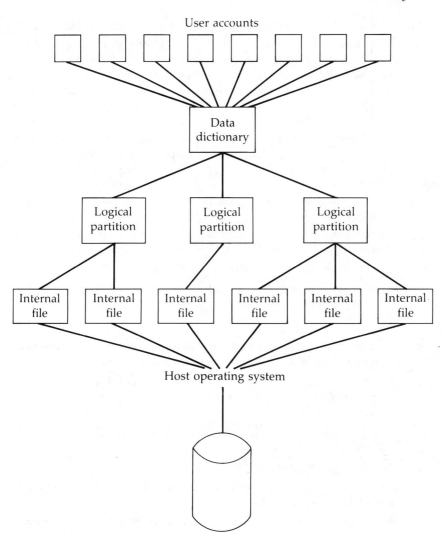

Figure 2.4 The layered architecture of Oracle Version 5.

rights and privileges are recorded in the Oracle Data Dictionary. This is a set of tables that provides a logical framework for the entire system. Only users with DBA status can see the data dictionary in its entirety. A user's view of the database is effectively defined by the information contained within the data dictionary.

At the internal level, the tables that comprise an Oracle database are stored in a series of files grouped into logical partitions. As well as the actual data in the tables, a certain amount of overhead information is encoded to enable the data to be stored in a relatively compressed format. The partitions are mapped to the underlying physical files which are stored and retrieved by the host machine's operating system, although it is possible in certain implementations for Oracle to by-pass the operating system and map the partitions directly to disk.

None of the actual physical organization of an Oracle database is visible from within an Oracle account, though it is possible to discover details of the internal logical organization of rows of data within a partition. Conversely, the logical grouping of the underlying database files into partitions is not apparent to the operating system.

Thus, an Oracle database can be said to adhere quite faithfully to the three-layer model for database systems (Figure 2.4). The external layer is represented by the views of the system presented by the individual user accounts, the conceptual layer is represented by the Oracle data dictionary and its mapping of the user tables to the logical partitions, and the internal layer is represented by the mapping of the partitions to the actual underlying operating system files.

Key points

- The interface between the users of a database and its physically stored data is best considered as a series of layers.

- Users' views of a database are logical views, each of which must be mapped to an underlying logical (conceptual) view of the whole system.

- The internal layer represents the mapping from the conceptual view to the physical storage. This may be performed via the underlying operating system of the host machine.

- The information content of an Oracle database is held in a series of one or more logical partitions.

- The mapping from a user's view to data in a partition is performed using data held in the Oracle Data Dictionary which is itself stored in the first (System) partition of a database.

- The mapping from the logical partitions to the physical file storage is performed via the host computer's operating system, though in many environments the Oracle software may be 'tuned' to perform this mapping directly.

EXERCISES

2.1 What are the fundamental purposes of the recommended three-layer model for database systems?

2.2 Describe and explain the function of each of the notional three layers of a database system:
(a) External layer,
(b) Internal layer,
(c) Conceptual layer.

2.3 In what ways does the Oracle Data Dictionary control an Oracle database?

2.4 An Oracle database is a layered system. How do the layers of an Oracle database correspond to the recommended three-layer model for databases?

2.5 Each piece of data stored in an Oracle database requires a certain amount of overhead information that is not visible to the user. Describe and explain the purpose of each piece of stored overhead information.

Reference

ANSI/SPARC (1978) *DBMS Framework: Report on the Study of Data Base Management Systems Information Systems* (Vol 3).

Three
An Introduction to SQL

A database management system requires a query language to enable its users to navigate their way through the files and data in a system. Structured Query Language (SQL) was developed simultaneously with the first prototype relational systems at the IBM research laboratories in the 1970s. It is a relationally complete language in that it provides the full functionality of the eight relational operations described in Chapter 1. In addition, it provides facilities to define tables and to enter, alter and delete the data within these tables.

The Oracle DBMS is completely built around the SQL language. SQL has itself become a *de facto* industry standard for relational systems. An ANSI standard (X3H2) now exists for SQL. However, this standard only addresses a subset of the facilities that most SQL-based systems provide, including IBM's own DB2. The Oracle Corporation have added their own extensions to SQL. This means that the hoped-for total compatibilty of software accross the various SQL-based systems does not exist in reality. There still remains, however, a large subset of Oracle's SQL that is directly compatible with most other systems, including DB2. This means that a large amount of software developed

(a) Customers

CUSTNO	CUSTNAME	ADDRESS
1	P. Jones	Leeds
2	A. Chan	Hong Kong
3	K. Green	Colombo
4	B. Smith	Leeds
5	A. Khan	

(b) Orders

ORDERNO	CUSTNO	ORDERDATE
1	1	24-JAN-86
2	1	31-JAN-86
3	2	04-FEB-86
4	4	12-FEB-86

(c) Orderlines

ORDERNO	STOCKNO	AMOUNT
1	1	55
1	3	124
2	1	24
2	2	35
2	3	12
2	4	125
2	5	33
3	1	45
3	2	12
3	3	234
3	4	13
3	5	145
4	4	32
4	5	125

(d) Stock

STOCKNO	SNAME	SPRICE	SLEVEL
1	Bolts	.15	250
2	Nuts	.75	6750
3	Nails	.65	4562
4	Spanners	4.76	135
5	Screws	.11	9875

Figure 3.1   Extended version of Customers/Stock/Orders database.

using the Oracle software can be used to access and process data held on other SQL-based sytems and vice versa.

Within this text, any Oracle command that is compatible with the DB2 implementation of SQL will be described as an SQL command. Any command that is unique to the Oracle system and thus not compatible with other systems will be highlighted. This chapter consists almost entirely of pure SQL commands.

There are two parts to the SQL language: the SQL Data Definition Language (DDL) and the SQL Data Manipulation Language (DML). The DDL is used to define tables in terms of the columns that they are comprised of and the types of data that these columns are allowed to hold. The DML is used to insert, extract, update and delete data in tables defined by the DDL.

Figure 3.1 shows an extended version of the Customers/Stock/ Orders database as introduced in the first chapter. In this chapter SQL will be used to build, query and alter this example database.

3.1 The SQL data definition language

3.1.1 Creating and altering a table

In order that a table may exist, it must first be Created. The SQL command Create is used to name a table and define its columns. A column requires a name and a *type*, the type indicating the domain of data values from which a column may draw its values.

In our table Customers as described in Chapter 1, there were three columns: CustNo, CustName, Address. Before defining this table, the kind of data values each of these columns may hold must be decided. Let us say that all CustNos are numeric with no fixed length, CustNames are word items which may be up to twenty characters long (including spaces), and Addresses are word items which may be up to forty characters long. The table would be defined thus in SQL:

```
Create Table Customers
2    (CustNo Integer Not Null,
3    CustName Char (20),
4    Address Char (40));
```

There are a number of points to note about this command. First of all, the line numbers. These are the result of entering a command in the SQL*Plus environment. Line numbers in themselves have no significance in SQL. They exist purely as markers within the text of a command. The programmer does not insert them. Every time the carriage return is pressed during the entry of a SQL command in the Oracle system, a line number is supplied. The semicolon at the end of the command indicates its termination, when the system attempts to execute it. As long as this table has not already been Created, the system should reply with the prompt:

```
Table Created
```

It is not necessary to spread SQL commands over a number of lines like this, but it is good practice: it renders the command more readable and it also makes the correction of mistakes easier. For convenience, and because they have no significance in SQL, the line numbers will be left out of all subsequent examples in this chapter.

As an aside, SQL*Plus commands are all single-line commands and thus do not require the semicolon to indicate their termination. Any Oracle command that requires a semicolon is therefore a SQL command, and consequently will usually be compatible with IBM's version of SQL.

The Create Table phrase is followed by the name of the table and then a set of brackets enclosing the column definitions. Each column is defined by its name and data type, with commas separating each definition. We defined CustNo as Integer Not Null. This means that every CustNo may only consist of a single number and that every row in the table must have a value for its CustNo. The use of Not Null forces this second restriction. This is our first step towards fabricating a form of entity integrity as described in Chapter 1. The other two columns are of type *char*, meaning that they can take any collection of characters for their values with the numbers in brackets indicating their maximum length. As there is no Not Null specification for these two columns, a row is allowed to have blank values for either or both of these.

A final point worth noting at this stage is the use of capital letters. Once again, these have only been used for convenience – SQL, when used in the Oracle environment, is not case sensitive. In other words, the entire command could have been entered in capitals or lower case and it would still have had the same effect. The only situation where the SQL *is* case sensitive is when assigning and comparing columns with char values. This will be described in greater detail in the section on the SQL DML.

The other tables described in Chapter 1 can also be Created thus:

```
Create Table Orders
      (OrderNo Integer Not Null,
      Custno Integer);
Create Table Stock
      (Stockno Integer Not Null,
      Sname Char (20),
      Sprice Number);
Create Table OrderLines
      (Orderno Integer Not Null,
      Stockno Integer Not Null,
      Amount Integer);
```

Notice that in Stock, Sprice was specified to be of type Number, not Integer. This is because the price of an item will be typically expressed as a decimal number indicating pounds and pence or dollars and cents, with the decimal part being restricted to two places of decimals. We may also wish to restrict its width. This cannot be done with columns of type Integer. If we wish to specify how many decimal places a Number may have, we need to Modify the definition given above. To specify that Sprice must be a number with two places of decimals after the point, the Alter Table command can be used thus:

```
Alter Table Stock
      Modify (SPrice Number(8,2));
```

This has changed the definition of Sprice from a number with an indeterminate number of decimal places to a number of no more than eight digits in length, with two digits being required after the decimal point. Modify may be used on any column in a table at any time where we have not reduced its width or attempted to change the type of data it holds. However, if it is used to reduce the width of a column or change its data type, it may only be used on columns with no data in them.

Alter Table can also be used to add columns to a table. In the extended version of the database, a new column – Slevel – has been added to the Stock table, indicating the level of an item in stock. To add this column to the table, we would say:

    Alter Table Stock
        Add (Slevel Integer);

Whereas Modify has constraints to its use, columns may be Added to a table at any time. Once added, though, a column cannot be removed.

It is also worth noting here that two Not Null columns were specified for the OrderLines table. This is because this table has a composite primary key consisting of OrderNo and StockNo, that is, each row will require values for both of these columns in order to differentiate it from all the other rows. Any number of columns in a table may be specified to be Not Null, and they do not have to be part of a candidate key for that table.

Another useful data type for Oracle tables is the *date type*. If it is required for a date to be assigned to each order in the Orders table, it could be done as follows:

    Alter Table Orders
        Add (Orderdate Date);

This adds a column Orderdate which accepts date values in the format DD-MMM-YY giving, for example, 24-Jan-86.

In order that the definition of a table may be checked, Oracle provides the SQL*Plus command Describe. For instance, the command:

    Describe Orders

will give:

Name	Null?	Type
ORDERNO	NOT NULL	INTEGER
CNO		INTEGER
ORDERDATE		DATE

As well as tables, SQL allows the creation of *views*. A view is a logical table that extracts its data from one or more underlying actual table. For instance, to create a view that was a subset of the Customers table that only consisted of those customers who lived in Leeds, the following command could be given:

```
Create View LeedsCustomers
      as
Select Custno, Custname
from Customers
where Address = 'Leeds';
```

In effect, this creates a new table based on data in another table. Any changes made to data in the underlying table will, of course, change the contents of the view. Once Created, a view can be treated by the SQL DML as if it were a real table for data extraction purposes. It can also be treated like a real table for update purposes as long as it is not built over more than one table (this is an Oracle restriction). Views will be discussed in detail in the SQL DML section as their effective creation requires understanding of the SQL Select command.

The Oracle data dictionary contains two tables, Tab and Views which hold the details of all tables and view definitions that belong to a user. These can be queried by the following commands:

```
Select * from Tab;
Select * from Views;
```

At this point, Select * can be taken to mean, informally, 'find everything'. The Select command will be discussed more fully in Section 3.2.2.

3.1.2   Index creation

An index is a useful device for speeding up access to rows within a table. With a book, it is quicker to look a subject up in an index rather than to read the whole book if you want to find those pages which have information on a certain topic. The same applies to files in a database. Records are usually retrieved from a file according to some search criteria such as *Find all Leeds Customers* or *Find the stock level for screws*. In these two cases, the relevant records would be retrieved from the given files more quickly if indexes were created over customer addresses and stock item names respectively. As mentioned in Chapter 2, when a table is Created, a default space is assigned to it within one of the logical partitions. A given amount (typically 10k) is set aside for the data in the table and an equal amount of space is set aside for indexes to be built over the data.

In order to create an index, you need to give the index a name, specify which table it is being created on and the columns over which it is being created. For instance, indexes into the Customers table based on address of customer and the Stock table based on stock item name would be set up thus:

      Create Index Caddress on Customers (Address);

or

      Create Index Itemname on Stock (Sname);

These two commands mean that a query such as

      Select Custname from Customers
      where Address = 'Hong Kong';

will cause the system to search the Address index on Customers first to discover the location of all Hong Kong records and then retrieve them. With large files consisting of many columns and thousands of rows, this will usually achieve a great saving in access time.

      The indexes above allow multiple values to exist in them, that is, there will be many entries for the same address or the same item name. However, it is possible to specify for item names to be unique if this is requested. It is especially useful for indexes built over those columns or sets of columns that comprise a candidate key for a table to have unique index item names. For instance, the following indexes could be created

      Create Unique Index Cno on Customers (Custno);

      Create Unique Index Ono on Orders (Orderno);

      Create Unique Index Sno on Stock (Stockno);

      Create Unique Index OSno on OrderLines (Orderno,Stockno);

      These four commands mean that not only have indexes been created over columns that comprise the primary key for each table, but also that there may be no duplicate entries for these key values. Any attempt to create a row in a table with a value that already exists in one of these unique indexes will result in an error message. These columns have already been specified as being not null – they must always contain a value for each row. Now it has been ensured that these values will also be unique to each row. By use of the Not Null and Unique Index commands, a form of entity integrity as described in Chapter 1 can be achieved, albeit indirectly. Note the final command. This creates a unique index over two columns, meaning that each combination of values for these two attributes in the OrderLines table must be unique – this is necessary for those tables with composite primary keys.

      A view is also provided in the Oracle Data Dictionary which gives details of all indexes created by the user. The command:

      Select * from Indexes;

will give the user information on the indexes they have created.

Although indexes speed up data access for large files, they slow down updates. If any changes are made to column values within a table over which an index has been built, corresponding changes will need to be made to the index. This means that it is not sensible to build indexes over column values that are liable to be changed frequently and involve a large number of rows in a given table, or over columns that will be seldom used as parameters for a search.

3.1.3   The Drop command

Drop is used to remove tables, views and indexes from an Oracle account. The command:

    Drop Table Customers;

will remove the Customers table from the system. Also, it means that the view LeedsCustomers is rendered inactive. Any attempt to extract data through this view will raise an error. However, the view definition will continue to exist. Thus, if the Customers table is re-created with those columns specified in the view definition (CustNo, CustName and Address) the view is rendered usable again. The view only ceases to exist when it is explicitly Dropped itself, as

    Drop View LeedsCustomers;

Indexes over a given table are automatically destroyed when the table they are built over is Dropped. Indexes may be removed independently of the tables that they index. So

    Drop Index Itemname;

will remove the index named Itemname which we built earlier over Sname in the Stock table.

3.1.4   Security

In a multi-user environment, it is desirable that users of an Oracle database have access to each others' tables. By default, no user has access to any other user's data (except for those users with DBA status – they have access to all the data in the system). To allow another user to use your data, you have to explicitly Grant them permission.

In SQL, there are four basic operations:

- Insert allows rows to be added to a table,
- Select extracts rows from a table,
- Delete removes rows from a table,
- Update changes rows within a table.

A user may Grant the use of any or all of these operations on any or all of their tables to other users. Suppose, for instance, we wished to give an Oracle user account called Jim the ability to look at the data in our Customers table. The command:

Grant Select On Customers To Jim;

will give Jim this ability. Jim will still not be able to add, remove or change rows in Customers. To do this, the relevant operations must be explicitly Granted to them. For example,

Grant Insert on Customers to Jim;

now gives Jim the power to add rows to our Customers table. If we wanted to give another user complete use of a table, we would say:

Grant All on Customers to June;

This gives June the ability to select, insert, update and delete rows in Customers. It also gives them the ability to create indexes and use the Alter Table commands on Customers.

The Revoke command is used to remove privileges from another user. For example, June's ability to be able to use the Alter Table or Update commands on Customers can be removed by the commands

Revoke Alter on Customers From June;
Revoke Update on Customers From June;

To remove all of Jim's privileges, we would say:

Revoke All on Customers From Jim;

By Granting a special user in Oracle called Public to carry out operations on our data, we allow all other Oracle users to have these privileges. For instance:

Grant Select, Insert on Stock to Public;

allows all other users of the system the ability to look at and add rows to the Stock table. Privileges can be Revoked from Public in the same way as they can from individual users.

The Oracle Data Dictionary contains a table called Systabauth which details all the access authorizations granted by or to a user. The command:

Select * from Systabauth;

will display this information.

3.2   The SQL data manipulation language

The data manipulation part of SQL consists of four basic commands: Insert, Select, Update and Delete. Each of these commands is used on row sets to produce row sets. (The version of Insert shown in this chapter only works with single row sets. The later chapter on SQL will show the use of Insert with multirow sets.) SQL has none of the loops or control structures associated with standard procedural-type programming languages. Instead, it is a *declarative* language: the programmer declares what the desired result of the program is and the system translates this into a series of actions. In the Oracle environment, SQL commands can be entered interactively or strung together in a file which can be called up by naming the file. In this chapter, the interactive mode will be used. The process of building command files will be described in the chapter on SQL*Plus.

3.2.1   The Insert command

Insert is used to enter rows into a table. The basic format of Insert is as follows:

> INSERT Into ***Name of table***
> Values
> (***Values for each column***);

Rows for the Customers table Created in the previous section can be built thus:

> Insert into Customers values (1,'P. Jones','Leeds');
> Insert into Customers values (2,'A. Chan','Hong Kong');
> Insert into Customers values (3,'K. Green','Colombo');
> Insert into Customers values (4,'B. Smith','Leeds');

These four commands have entered four rows into the Customers table. The value assigned to each column is separated from the value for the next column by a comma. The values are assigned to columns in the order in which they were declared in the Create command. Thus, in the first row, 1 was assigned to the CustNo, P. Jones was assigned to the CustName and Leeds was assigned to the Address. The single quotation marks are placed around the latter column values because they are of type *char*. Failure to use the quotation marks would cause an error to be raised by the system. Numeric type column values do not require the quotation marks.

The Stock table was Created with three attributes (StockNo, SName, Sprice) and then had one (SLevel) Added to it. Rows can be entered thus:

    Insert into Stock Values (1,'Bolts',0.15,250);
    Insert into Stock Values (2,'Nuts',0.75,6750);
    Insert into Stock Values (3,'Nails',0.65,4562);
    Insert into Stock Values (4,'Spanners',4.76,135);
    Insert into Stock Values (5,'Screws',0.11,9875);

Note how, in this set of commands, the third column value, Sprice, had to have two numbers assigned after the decimal point each time. This would be necessary even if the price was a whole value, because we Modifyed the definition of Sprice to Number(8,2), so a whole number such as 10 would need to be entered as 10.00.

Due to the Unique indexes that were Created over certain columns, the system constantly checks for duplicate values in these columns. For instance, the Orders table had a Unique index Created over the OrderNo column. Therefore these two commands would raise an error message:

    Insert into Orders Values (1,1,'24-Jan-86');
    Insert into Orders Values (1,1,'31-Jan-86');

The second of these commands would result in an error message being displayed to the user because a row with an OrderNo of 1 has already been entered by the first command. The second row will not be written into the table. Assigning of value 1 to the CustNo in the second command is legal as CustNos has not been specified as unique for the Orders table. Thus, the command

    Insert into Orders Values (2,1,'31-Jan-86');

is acceptable. More rows can be entered thus:

    Insert into Orders Values (3,2,'4-Feb-86');
    Insert into Orders Values (4,4,'12-Feb-86');

As described in Section 3.1.1, the OrderDate column is a date type column with the format DD-MMM-YY. Because there are alphabetic characters involved, the Oracle software requires the single quotation marks around date values.

Our final table is the OrderLines table. This has three integer type columns: OrderNo, StockNo, and Amount. There is a unique index over OrderNo and StockNo. Because this is a composite index, OrderNos and StockNos may be repeated over a number of rows. It is the combination of OrderNo and StockNo in each row that has to be unique. Therefore, the following Insert commands are acceptable:

```
Insert into OrderLines Values (1,1,55);
Insert into OrderLines Values (1,3,124);
Insert into OrderLines Values (2,1,24);
Insert into OrderLines Values (2,2,35);
Insert into OrderLines Values (2,3,12);
```

and so on.

It is worth noting here that, although the rows have been entered in ascending key column order, this is not a requirement of SQL, it has been done simply for convenience. Rows can be entered in random order and are, by default, displayed in the order in which they are entered. It is possible to change the order in which they are displayed – how to do this will be explained in the later chapter on SQL.

In all the examples above, a variant of the Insert command was used that assigns the column values for an entire row. It is possible to assign values to some of the columns only. In our extended database, we have a new Customer (A. Khan) with no address. To enter this row, we can simply say:

```
Insert into Customers
    (CustNo,Custname)
    Values
    (5,'A. Khan');
```

In this format, as values are not being assigned to every column in the table, those columns that are assigned values need to be specified. Thus on line 2, we designate CustNo and CustName as the columns into which data is being inserted. The values on line 4 are assigned in this specified column order.

The statement above is perfectly legal as the Address column is allowed to accept null values. However, it would not be legal to do this:

```
Insert into Customers
    (CustName, Address)
    Values
    ('F. Peters','Hong Kong');
```

because it is not possible to add a row without a CustNo value. Our Create command for this table specified that CustNo is not allowed to accept null values, thus every time Insert is used on this table, a value must be assigned to CustNo. In the same way,

```
Insert into OrderLines
      (OrderNo, StockNo)
      Values
      (6,5);
```

is acceptable, but

```
Insert into OrderLines
      (StockNo, Amount)
      Values
      (5,245);
```

is not as there is no value assigned to the not null column OrderNo. Incidentally, if the Oracle DBMS had automatic referential integrity, the first of these two Insert commands would also be illegal because it assigns a value (5) to OrderNo. OrderNo is the key for Orders, and 5 does not exist as an OrderNo value in this table.

For large numbers of records, the Insert command quickly becomes tiresome to use. The SQL*Forms tool enables rapid entry of large numbers of rows into a table that has been Created in SQL*Plus.

3.2.2 The Select command

The SQL command Select is used for extracting and displaying the data contents of tables. It provides the full functionality of the eight relational operations: SELECT, PROJECT, JOIN, UNION, INTERSECT, MINUS, TIMES and DIVIDE. Confusingly, therefore, Select does not mean the same thing as the basic relational SELECT operation. Most of the above operations are achieved quite simply as the following text will demonstrate.

3.2.2.1 SELECT *operations*
The relational SELECT operation extracts specified rows from a given table. All SQL Select commands take the same basic format:

```
Select     ***the data you want to select***
From       ***the tables holding the data***
Where      ***any conditions that the data has to satisfy***
```

The relational SELECT operation is achievable in SQL by the command SELECT * followed by the name of the appropriate table. Thus, the command:

```
Select * From Customers;
```

will give the output indicated in Table 3.1.

Table 3.1   Unrestricted Select on Customers.

CUSTNO	CUSTNAME	ADDRESS
1	P. Jones	Leeds
2	A. Chan	Hong Kong
3	K. Green	Colombo
4	B. Smith	Leeds
5	A. Khan	

Select * causes all the column values for all the rows in a table to be displayed. The selection may be narrowed down so

    Select * from Customers
        where Address = 'Leeds';

will give:

CUSTNO	CUSTNAME	ADDRESS
1	P. Jones	Leeds
4	B. Smith	Leeds

In the second line of the above command, we put quotation marks around the word 'Leeds' because it is a char type column. This is the one situation where the Oracle software is case sensitive. Had 'leeds' or the 'LEEDS' been entered within the quotation marks, no rows would have been retrieved as there are no rows in the Customers table with these exact literal values for Address.

Selects may be made over a number of conditions. For example,

    Select * from Customers
    where Address = 'Leeds'
        and Custno > 1;

will give

CUSTNO	CUSTNAME	ADDRESS
4	B. Smith	Leeds

This last command effectively told the system to 'find all the rows in the Customers table whose Address is equal to Leeds and whose CustNo is greater than 1'. The full range of the standard logical operators (*AND, OR, NOT*) and comparators (>,=,<,>=,<=,<>) may be used in Where expressions. There are further special SQL logical operators which will be introduced at later stages in the text.

Earlier on, a view called LeedsCustomers was defined which was essentially a subset of the Customers table. This view can be treated as an actual table for Select purposes. The command:

    Select * from LeedsCustomers;

will give

```
CUSTNO   CUSTNAME
---------------------
      1   P. Jones
      4   B. Smith
```

In this case, the Address column is not displayed because it was not specified as part of the original view definition. The view definition was essentially a PROJECTION and a SELECTION over two of the columns in the Customers table: CustNo and CustName.

3.2.2.2   PROJECT *operations*

The relational PROJECT operation extracts the different values assigned to a column within a table. For instance, a PROJECT over the CustNo values in the Customers table will yield the numbers 1, 2, 3 and 4. This can be achieved by specifying column names in the Select command, so

    Select Custno
    from Customers;

will give

```
CUSTNO
--------
      1
      2
      3
      4
```

The use of Select in this way may yield duplicate values. The command

    Select Address
    from Customers;

will give

```
ADDRESS
-----------
Leeds
Hong Kong
Colombo
Leeds
```

Strictly speaking, this is not a true PROJECT, as it has yielded a table with a duplicate row. This can be removed by a variant of the Select command thus:

```
Select Distinct Address
from Customers;
```

which gives

```
ADDRESS
-----------
Leeds
Colombo
Hong Kong
```

The use of Distinct constrains each instance of output, that is, each row, to be unique. A PROJECT can be implemented over more than one column. For example, the command

```
Select Custname, Address
from Customers;
```

will give

```
CUSTNAME    ADDRESS
------------------------
P. Jones    Leeds
A. Chan     Hong Kong
K. Green    Colombo
B. Smith    Leeds
A. Khan
```

The Where clause can also be used with these simple projections. The command:

```
Select Custno, Custname
from Customers
where Address <> 'Leeds';
```

for example, constitutes a request for all Customers who do not have an address equal to Leeds to be listed, and thus gives:

```
CUSTNO   CUSTNAME
---------------------
     2   A. Chan
     3   K. Green
```

A. Khan is not produced in this output, even though their address is not 'Leeds'. This is because they have a null value for their address. Null is a special value in SQL; it is not equal to anything. Being not equal to anything, it has no value and cannot be used in comparison with any other value. Thus it is neither equal nor not equal to anything!

The Distinct clause constrains all rows to be unique in the output from a Select command. Thus duplicate values for columns may still appear from a Select Distinct command implemented over more than one column. For instance, the command:

```
Select Distinct Address, Custname
from Customers;
```

will give

```
ADDRESS      CUSTNAME
-------------------------
Leeds        B. Smith
Leeds        P. Jones
Colombo      K. Green
Hong Kong    A. Chan
             A. Khan
```

Leeds appears in the Address column more than once because there is more than one Customer with that Address. The criteria for a PROJECT operation is still satisfied because there are no duplicate rows in the output.

3.2.2.3 JOIN *operations*

The ability to JOIN tables over common attribute values is fundamental to relational systems. In SQL, this is achieved by comparing values held under a column in one table with values held under a column in a different table. For instance, to find the names and addresses of all Customers who have placed orders, we need to JOIN the rows in the Customers table with those in the Orders table which have the same CustNo value. This is achieved thus:

```
Select CustName, Address, OrderNo
from Customers, Orders
where Customers.CustNo = Orders.CustNo;
```

This will give:

```
CUSTNAME   ADDRESS     ORDERNO
-------------------------------------
P. Jones   Leeds           1
P. Jones   Leeds           2
A. Chan    Hong Kong       3
B. Smith   Leeds           4
```

Thus, for each Order, the corresponding customer's name and address has been matched using the CustNo column common to both tables. Note the absence of any output for customers Green and Khan. This is because their CustNo does not appear in the Orders table. JOINs can be implemented simultaneously over a number of tables. To find out what was on these orders, a JOIN would have to be made with the OrderLines table. This can be done over the OrderNo column which is common to the Orders and OrderLines tables thus:

```
Select Orders.Orderno, CustName, Address, StockNo, Amount
from Customers, Orders, OrderLines
where Customers.CustNo = Orders.CustNo
    and Orders.OrderNo = OrderLines.OrderNo;
```

This will give the output indicated in Table 3.2.

This command has therefore generated a customer's name and address for each item ordered from stock by cross-relating by means of JOINs from the OrderLines to the Customers via the Orders table. In the Select command, the OrderNo column had to be qualified by adding the name of the table, writing it as Orders.OrderNo. This had to be done in order to output values from a column that appears in more than one table in the From clause. When this happens, SQL requires the user to specify which table the column values are to be drawn from.

In the output given in Table 3.2, the width of the columns was such that each line of output had to be spread over two lines; this makes it difficult to read. In the chapter on SQL*Plus, those commands provided by Oracle that enable the output from tables to be presented in a more readable form than that allowed by standard SQL. Another feature of this output is that the names and addresses of customers are repeated for every order item within each order. This can be eliminated by the Oracle SQL*Plus command Break On. In this instance, the command:

```
Break On OrderNo On CustName On Address
```

Table 3.2   A 3-table JOIN.

ORDERNO	CUSTNAME	ADDRESS
STOCKNO	AMOUNT	
1	P. Jones	Leeds
1	55	
1	P. Jones	Leeds
3	124	
2	P. Jones	Leeds
1	24	
2	P. Jones	Leeds
2	35	
2	P. Jones	Leeds
3	12	
2	P. Jones	Leeds
4	125	
2	P. Jones	Leeds
5	33	
3	A. Chan	Hong Kong
1	45	
3	A. Chan	Hong Kong
2	12	
3	A. Chan	Hong Kong
3	234	
3	A. Chan	Hong Kong
4	13	
3	A. Chan	Hong Kong
5	145	
4	B. Smith	Leeds
4	32	
4	B. Smith	Leeds
5	125	

means that if the above command were to be repeated, the values under OrderNo, CustName and Address will only be displayed when they change. There is an order of priority in these Breaks. Because OrderNo was named first, the CustName P. Jones and Address Leeds will re-appear when the OrderNo changes. Breaks and column definitions will be discussed further in the chapter on SQL*Plus.

To incorporate the names and prices of items into this output, it would have to be JOINed with the item names and prices in the Stock table based on the StockNo column common to Stock and OrderLines:

```
Select Orders.OrderNo, CustName, Address,
Stock.StockNo, Sname, Amount, Sprice
from Customers, Orders, OrderLines, Stock
where Customers.CustNo = Orders.CustNo
    and Orders.OrderNo = OrderLines.OrderNo
    and OrderLines.StockNo = Stock.StockNo;
```

Once again, Stock.StockNo has had to have been specified in the Select part as a column that appears in two tables has been requested to be displayed. This command would extract all the details necessary to compile a set of order notes based on the data held in the four tables. It would be cumbersome to have to enter this command every time this information was required. It would be better to Create a view instead using the following command:

```
Create View OrderNotes
      As
Select Orders.OrderNo, CustName, Address,
Stock.StockNo, SName, Amount, SPrice
from Customers, Orders, OrderLines, Stock
where Customers.Custno = Orders.Custno
      and Orders.Orderno = OrderLines.Orderno
      and OrderLines.Stockno = Stock.Stockno;
```

Once this view has been Created the information can be retrieved simply by saying:

```
Select * from Ordernotes;
```

3.2.2.4   UNION, INTERSECT *and* MINUS *operations*

SQL provides these operators explicitly. They can be used over any compatible sets of rows. In other words, the rows do not have to be extracted from within the same table or view. What is required is that they have they same number of columns and that these columns are of the same data types.

Suppose, for example, that it was necessary to find out the names and addresses of all customers who had ordered bolts and all customers who had ordered screws. This can be achieved by Selecting from the view OrderNotes all CustNames and Addresses for orders for screws and carrying out a Union with all CustNames and Addresses for orders for bolts. This can be programmed thus:

```
Select Custname, Address
from Ordernotes
where SName = 'Screws'
Union
Select CustName, Address
from OrderNotes
where SName = 'Bolts';
```

This will give the following output:

```
CustName   Address
------------------------
B. Smith   Leeds
A. Chan    Hong Kong
P. Jones   Leeds
```

This is because Chan and Jones have placed orders for screws and Smith, Chan and Jones have placed orders for bolts. The UNION of these two sets of rows is Smith, Chan and Jones. The INTERSECTion of these two sets of rows would yield only those customers who have ordered both bolts and screws. This is achieved thus:

```
Select CustName, Address
from OrderNotes
where Sname = 'Screws'
Intersect
Select CustName, Address
from OrderNotes
where Sname = 'Bolts';
```

giving

```
CUSTNAME   ADDRESS
------------------------
A. Chan    Hong Kong
P. Jones   Leeds
```

If the word Intersect were to be replaced in line four of the command above with the word Minus those customers who have ordered screws and not ordered bolts would be listed. In this case, the output would be:

```
No records selected
```

as there are no rows that actually match this criteria. However, if the command

> Select Custname, Address
> from Ordernotes
> where Sname = 'Bolts'
> Minus
> Select Custname, Address
> from Ordernotes
> where Sname = 'Screws';

were given instead, we would be asking for those who have ordered bolts and not screws, and the result would be:

```
CUSTNAME   ADDRESS
-----------------------
B. Smith      Leeds
```

This is a feature of the basic set operators. UNION and INTERSECT are commutative, that is, it does not matter which order you give the arguments to the operation, you get the same result. MINUS is not: by reversing the order of the arguments, you get a different result.

3.2.2.5   *TIMES*

The TIMES operation is achieved quite simply in SQL. Being the Cartesian product of two sets of rows, it can be achieved in SQL simply by programming an unconditional JOIN. For instance, to match all customer names against all stock item names, the command

> Select Custname, Sname
> from Customers, Stock;

could be given. As there is no condition in this JOIN, all rows from customers will be matched against all rows in stock as shown in Table 3.3.

3.2.2.6   *DIVIDE*

Whereas the other seven relational operations are relatively easy to implement in SQL, the DIVIDE operation is difficult. This is not a serious problem as it is required only very rarely. The vast majority of queries in a given system will involve SELECT, PROJECT and JOIN operations.

DIVIDE is, in itself, a composite operation in that it implicitly involves the SELECT, PROJECT, JOIN and MINUS operations. When one set of tuples is divided by another, one is looking to yield the set of values held in the non-overlapping columns belonging to the first set that are

Table 3.3 Stock TIMES Customers.

CUSTNAME	SNAME
P. Jones	Bolts
P. Jones	Nuts
P. Jones	Nails
P. Jones	Spanners
P. Jones	Screws
A. Chan	Bolts
A. Chan	Nuts
A. Chan	Nails
A. Chan	Spanners
A. Chan	Screws
K. Green	Bolts
K. Green	Nuts
K. Green	Nails
K. Green	Spanners
K. Green	Screws
B. Smith	Bolts
B. Smith	Nuts
B. Smith	Nails
B. Smith	Spanners
B. Smith	Screws
A. Khan	Bolts
A. Khan	Nuts
A. Khan	Nails
A. Khan	Spanners
A. Khan	Screws

paired against all the column values in the second. For instance, to find those orders which have been placed against all the items in the stock file, we could take one set of rows consisting of the OrderNo and StockNo combinations in the OrderLines table and divide it by another set of rows consisting of all the StockNos in the Stock table. This would yield those OrderNos which are placed against all the StockNos. In SQL, this has to be expressed in a slightly convoluted way by selecting all the OrderNos in the OrderLines table such that there is no StockNo in the Stock table that they are not matched against! How this can be coded is described in detail in Chapter 6. At this stage, it is sufficient to say that it can be coded from within SQL itself, without recourse to any non-standard constructs.

3.2.3 The Update command

Update is used to change values in rows that have already been Inserted. The basic form of the Update command is

> Update ***name the table***
> Set   ***assign new values to certain columns***
> Where ***for all those rows satisfying these conditions***

For instance, there is a row in the Customers table without an address. If we wished to enter an address in this row, we could do so using the following command:

> Update Customers
> Set Address = 'Hong Kong'
> where Custname = 'A. Khan';

Changing an existing value is done in a similar way. So to change the name 'bolts' in the Stock table to 'half-inch bolts' for example, the following command would be used:

> Update Stock
> Set Sname = 'Half-Inch Bolts'
> where Sname = 'Bolts';

Like the other basic SQL operators, Update is a set-level operator. That is, it is activated on the entire set of records that meet a given condition, not just the first. This means that if there were more than one row in the Stock table with the name 'Bolts', these other rows would also have had their name changed to 'Half-Inch Bolts'.

Updates can also be unconditional. To increase all the prices in the stock table by 10 per cent, the following commands could be used:

> Update Stock
> Set SPrice = SPrice * 1.10;

To put a limit for all orders against Stock Item 2 of no more than 10, a compound condition as follows would achieve the desired result.

> Update OrderLines
> Set Amount = 10
> where Stockno = 2
> and Amount > 10;

This restricts the update to those orders against Stock item 2 whose order amount exceeds 10. Without the second part of the condition, the command would have changed the order amount to 10 even if less than 10 had been requested.

3.2.4 The Delete command

The Delete command is used to remove rows from a table. It does not affect the definition of a table. Thus, all the rows may be removed from a table by Delete, but the table will continue to exist until it has been Dropped. Deletes may be conditional. For example:

> Delete from Customers
> where Address = 'Colombo';

removes all those customers whose address is Colombo.

> Delete from Customers;

removes all rows from the Customers table. Delete should, of course, be used with care.

3.3 Summary

The purpose of this chapter has been to demonstrate the relationally complete nature of SQL. There is a lot more to SQL than outlined here. SQL provides many extra query processing facilities, including some commands for processing as well as extracting the data held in tables. These will be addressed in Chapter 6. Already in this chapter, some facilities have been described that are not available in the ANSI standard SQL, but except where features have been explicitly pointed out as being available only in SQL*Plus, there is nothing here that will not be found in the vast majority of 'true' SQL-based systems.

Key points

- The Oracle DBMS is built around SQL, which is the *de facto* industry standard language for relational database management systems.
- SQL has two parts: the SQL data definition language (DDL) for defining relational data structures and the SQL data manipulation language (DML) for updating and querying relational data structures.
- The SQL DML has four basic operators: Insert, Delete, Update and Select.
- The functionality of all eight of the basic relational algebraic operations is subsumed into the SQL Select operator. As such, SQL can be regarded as a relationally complete language.

EXERCISES

3.1 Specify the SQL statements necessary to execute the following algebraic operations:
   (a) SELECT Orders where Stockno = 3
   (b) PROJECT Stock (Sname)
   (c) JOIN Stock, OrderLines (Stockno)
   (d) Stock TIMES Orders.

3.2 Using the database in Figure 3.1, what would be the output from the following SQL statements:
   (a) Select * from Stock;
   (b) Select Distinct OrderNo from OrderLines;
   (c) Select Orderno, Address
       from Customers, Orders
       where Customers.Custno = Orders.Custno;
   (d) Select Orderno
       from OrderLines
       where Stockno = 1
       Union
       Select Orderno from OrderLines
       where Stockno = 3;
   (e) Select Custno, Orderno
       from Customers, Orders;
   (f) Select Orderno
       from OrderLines
       where Stockno = 1
       Minus
       Select Orderno from OrderLines
       where Stockno = 3;
   (g) Select Orderno
       from OrderLines
       where Stockno = 3
       Intersect
       Select Orderno from OrderLines
       where Stockno = 1;

3.3 For each of the statements above, specify the algebraic operation(s) that is being activated.

3.4 What are the differences between a *view* and a *table*?

PART TWO
Developing Applications with Oracle

Four
The SQL*Plus Environment

4.1 The user's view of the SQL*Plus environment	SQL*Plus software
	Key points
4.2 Report generation using	Exercises

The SQL language allows data in relational tables to be created and manipulated. It has nothing to say about the actual environment in which this data is used. A database user requires functionality additional to that provided by SQL. For instance, users need to be able to edit, save and recall their SQL commands; they need to process and re-format the data into a more readable form; they need to enter messages and prompts to other users and so on.

In more traditional systems, this functionality was achieved by allowing the commands of the database query language to be embedded within a high-level language such as COBOL or FORTRAN. Thus the high-level language would take care of the user dialogue and the processing and presentation of the data while the data query language would take care of the access to the data itself. This option is available in the Oracle environment. On most machines where Oracle software is implemented, it is possible to acquire a range of pre-compilers that allow SQL commands to be embedded within a more traditional high-level language. In fact, the X3H2 ANSI SQL standard assumes this to be the norm and concentrates specifically on the interface between SQL and other languages.

Although support for this approach is provided by the Oracle software, the manufacturers' basic philosophy is to render it redundant. They aim instead to provide as complete a data processing environment as possible by means of a number of additional software tools such as SQL*Forms and SQL*Report and by significantly extending the SQL language itself. In this chapter, some of the main extensions that the Oracle Corporation have made to SQL will be examined. Most of what is described herein is unique to the Oracle environment and will not work on other SQL-based systems.

The SQL*Plus software is intended to render SQL more usable and versatile. For convenience, SQL*Plus extensions will be considered within two categories: those that effect the SQL*Plus environment for the user, and those that provide extra data processing and report-formating facilities.

4.1   The user's view of the SQL*Plus environment

4.1.1   The Set command

When executing an SQL command, the output may frequently contain more lines than the screen can display. Some of the commands in the previous chapter will have generated more than a screenful of data. When this happens, the system displays data by scrolling without pausing between one screenful and the next. This, of course, can be very annoying! The following command will almost certainly generate more than a screenful of data on most systems.

Select * from Dtab;

The Dtab table (the table that indexes the Oracle Data Dictionary) has 44 entries in it, each filling a line on a standard screen of 80 characters width. As most computer screens display around 25 lines at a time, the first 19 lines of output from this table will be lost 'off the top' of the screen. The Set command can be used to overcome this.

To force a pause in the output from a screen, you must first decide on a prompt to give to the user before each page of output. A sensible prompt would be one to hit the carriage return as this is what has to be done to get any output once a pause has been Set. This prompt can be set thus:

Set Pause HitReturn

A pause will now be forced before each page of output by switching this on thus:

Set Pause On

Now when the SQL command above is entered (or any other SQL command for that matter), before any output appears, the prompt

HitReturn appears on the screen. Once the carriage return has been depressed, a page of output appears. If there is any more, the prompt appears again and another page appears and so on.

There is a default of 14 lines for a page of output in Oracle. This can be changed. If for instance, one prefers to see 20 lines of data at a time, the command

    Set PageSize 20

will have this effect. By default also, the Oracle software outputs 1 blank line between each page. This can also be changed. The command

    Set NewPage 6

will cause 6 blank lines to be output between each page. Set NewPage 0 will clear the screen between each page on most terminals.

If the output is to a printer, one does not usually require pauses. These can be cancelled with the command

    Set Pause Off

Similarly, PageSize and NewPage can be reset at any time. For output that is to be directed to a printer, a PageSize of 65 lines is usually appropriate for A4 sized paper. There are many other parameters that Set can be used to effect the user's working environment, some of which will be discussed at appropriate times.

4.1.2 Saving and editing commands

One of the most fundamental activities to a programmer is the ability to save and edit programs. Consider the following SQL command:

    Select Custname, Orderno
    2   from Customers, Orders
    3   where Address = 'Leeds'
    4   and Customer.Custno = Orders.Custno;

This would retrieve the names of all the customers who lived in Leeds and who had placed an order along with the number of each order placed. It would be inconvenient to have to type this entire command in every time we wanted this piece of information. This is not, in fact, necessary. The SQL*Plus commands Save, Get, Run and Start give various ways around this.

When the above command is entered – on receiving the semicolon and final carriage return – the system will attempt to execute it. The command is now in what is called the *SQL buffer*. The SQL buffer always contains the most recently entered SQL command. It can be activated at any time with the SQL*Plus command Run. Thus if one wants to repeat a command, entering Run will achieve this, and will continue to do so until another command has been entered. The contents of the SQL buffer can be written to disk by use of the Save command and thus will not be lost when it is over-written by another command. When using Save, a name must be given to the command. With the above command:

Save LeedsOrders

will cause the contents of the SQL buffer to be written to disk with the name 'LeedsOrders'. Other commands can now be executed, each one over-writing the previous one in the SQL buffer. If we wish to recall the above command, the instruction

Get LeedsOrders

will read it back from disk and place it in the SQL buffer. It can then be executed with the Run instruction. Alternatively, the instruction

Start LeedsOrders

will place the command in the buffer and execute it immediately. Get would be used if, for some reason, the command was not to be executed immediately. This may be because it needs to be edited first. SQL*Plus provides the following instructions that allow the user to edit the contents of the SQL buffer:

l	List the contents of the SQL buffer
l<*n*>	List line n of the SQL buffer
DEL	Delete the most recently listed line
i	Insert text after the most recently listed line
c	Change text in the most recently listed line
a	Append to the SQL buffer

In the following section, the examples given involve dialogue with the system and user input will be in *italic* type, whereas responses from the system will not.

Suppose the output from LeedsOrders needed to be restricted to those customers whose name fell in the second half of the alphabet. This would require the addition of the line and Custname > 'M'. With the above command in the SQL buffer, the entry of the instruction 'i' will result in the system displaying the number 5 and awaiting the input of an extra line. Thus the sequence of instructions

i
5   *and Custname > 'M';*

will change the output accordingly. Having changed the contents of the SQL buffer thus, the l instruction will now list five lines rather than four. Note that this has amended the contents of the buffer, *not* the original LeedsCustomers command. To change the contents of the Saved command, it has to be over-written with an explicit Save, using the same file name as before. Use of the Save command with a different file name will cause a separate file to be Saved containing the altered instruction.

To drop the last line of this command, the instruction Del would achieve this. Del deletes the most recently listed line. Thus, using the l instruction to list the entire buffer, followed by the Del instruction will cause the last line to be deleted. To delete any other line, the line number to be deleted must be specified and then give the Del instruction. For instance, the command

> *l3*

will give the response

> 3   where Address = Leeds

To use the Del instruction now would cause this line to be deleted from the buffer. However, use of the RUN command to execute this command would produce an error message from the system as the syntax of the SQL command would now be in error. To restore the Where part of the command, it has to be re-inserted after line 2. The i instruction always inserts after the most recently listed line, thus the following sequence of instructions would now be necessary:

> *l2*
> 2   from Customers, Orders
> *i*
> 3   *where Address = Leeds*

The Run command will now give the same output as before. To change the output from Leeds to Colombo customers, line 3 has to be changed from Leeds to Colombo. This can be achieved thus:

> *l3*
> 3   where Address = Leeds
> *c/Leeds/Colombo*

The l instruction will now show line 3 amended accordingly and the Run instruction will now output the Colombo rather than the Leeds orders. This has effectively created a new command which can be Saved. In the example above, l was used to list the line to be edited and C was used to change it. A simplified syntax of C is thus:

> c/oldphrase/newphrase

The system scans the line for the first instance of the specified old phrase and replaces it with the new version.

Saveing, Running and editing the SQL buffer is appropriate for single SQL commands. However, there are many situations when the user will wish to Save and Run whole sequences of commands, including SQL*Plus commands. This can be achieved by setting a non-SQL buffer for input of a sequence of instructions.

Suppose we wished to display all Orders from Leeds followed by all Orders from Colombo with a pause between each set of orders. This involves two separate SQL Select commands along with a sequence of SQL*Plus Set Pause commands. To string these together into a single command file, we need to set up a non-SQL buffer and then input into and save from this buffer thus:

> *Set Buffer A*
> *Input*
> 1   *Set Pause 'Hit Return for Colombo Orders'*
> 2   *Set Pause Off*
> 3   *Select * from OrderNotes*
> 4   *where Address = 'Leeds';*
> 5   *SET PAUSE ON*
> 6   *Select * from OrderNotes*
> 7   *where Address = 'Colombo';*
> 8   *SET PAUSE OFF*
> 9   (Press Carriage Return at this point)
> *Save*   *LeedsandColombo*
> Wrote file LeedsandColombo
> *Start*   *LeedsandColombo*

The above sequence of commands will cause the output as specified above. The Set Buffer A instruction informs the system that we wish to set up a non-SQL buffer called 'A'. The Input instruction informs the system that the next sequence of commands are to be written to this buffer and *not* the SQL buffer. Because they are going to an alternative buffer, Oracle will not attempt to execute the commands immediately they have been input. The system will now respond with a sequence of line numbers against which a series of SQL and SQL*Plus commands can be entered. When these commands have been entered, the Save instruction will cause them to be written to disk and the Start instruction will enable them to be read back from the disk and executed.

Start rather than Get is necessary here because there is more than one SQL command in the file as well as some SQL*Plus commands. Attempting to load a SQL*Plus command into the SQL buffer will cause an error, as would attempting to load more than one SQL command at a time. Get takes a file and attempts to load its entire contents into the SQL buffer, whereas Start causes the system to read the file sequentially and to execute each line as it comes to it. SQL commands are loaded into the buffer as and when they are encountered. Thus, at the end of the execution of the above command file, the l instruction will list the last Select command in the file as this will have been the command most recently loaded into the SQL buffer.

The contents of a non-SQL buffer cannot be edited within the Oracle software. Instead, the editor provided by the host system has to be used. The SQL*Plus command Edit does this automatically. For instance, on Unix-based machines, the command

Edit LeedsandManchester

will call up the Unix text editor 'ed' with the saved file Leedsand-Manchester as the material to be edited. It is possible to use other editors than the one provided by the system. There are two ways of doing this: changing the default editor or calling up a different editor from the host operating system.

The SQL*Plus command Define can be used to change a number of parameters, including the default editor. For instance, if, in Unix, the user wished to invoke the window editor 'vi' rather than the line editor 'ed', the command:

Define_Editor = 'vi'

will cause 'vi' to be called up next time the Edit command is used.

It is possible to invoke an operating system command external to the Oracle software. On a Unix system, for example, a Unix command can be called up at any time by use of the ! sign followed by the desired command. (This is operating system dependent. In VMS, for instance, it is usually the '$' sign.) Thus, if you wished to call up a word proccessing package that was resident on your system without necessarily making this the default editor you can instead call it directly from the Oracle system. For instance, a user of an IBM-PC compatible who had WordStar on their system could edit their command files with the command:

!ws LeedsandManchester.sql

Note that, in this instance, the suffix .sql was added onto the name of the file to be edited. When Oracle writes a command file to disk, the .sql suffix is, by default, automatically placed on its name. When using the default editor from the Edit command, this suffix is assumed. Invoking a host system command with the ! (or $) symbol means that the .sql suffix has to be specified because the host computer's operating system will not assume that it should be there and would thus not be able to find the file. When using a word processing package, it is important to edit the command file in *non-document* mode. When the editor or word processor invoked is exited, the user is returned immediately to Oracle.

This facility to access the operating system is a useful feature of Oracle. For instance, to list all the Oracle command files saved on disk, the appropriate system listing command should be used. For instance, in Unix, the command:

    !ls *.sql

will list all files in the current directory with the .sql suffix which are thus Oracle command files. The equivalent command on an IBM-PC would be

    !dir *.sql

.sql is the default suffix placed onto SQL*Plus command files. The SET command can be used to change this. For instance, the command

    Set Suffix orafile

will cause the Oracle software to assume the suffix orafile to be the default extension to SQL*Plus command files. Note that it is not possible to list details of tables Created in Oracle from within the operating system. These can only be accessed from within Oracle with the SQL command:

    Select * from Catalog;

4.1.3   Obtaining hard copy output

SQL*Plus provides an interactive environment whereby commands are entered, interpreted by the system and executed immediately, with the output being sent to the screen on which they were entered. It is frequently the case that a printed copy of the output is required. This is done in Oracle by use of the SQL*Plus-command, Spool.

The Spool command is used to set up a file to write all of the output from the screen to an external file. It is then used to close that file and, optionally, to print it on the host printer. For instance, a sequence of commands to send the output generated by the Saved command file LeedsCustomers the printer will be as follows:

    Spool   ListOfLeedsCustomers
    Start   LeedsCustomers
    Spool   out

The first Spool command sets up a name for the spool file. From now on, all data output to the screen will also be written to an external file with this name until another Spool command is entered. Spool out closes the spool file and sends its contents directly to the system printer. It will still exist on the system with the .lst suffix automatically placed on it. (This suffix varies from one operating system to another.) Spool off could have been used. This closes the spool file without printing it out. It may be printed out, re-displayed or edited when the system has been Exited, or by use of the ! sign followed by the appropriate host system command.

4.2 Report generation using SQL*Plus software

The SQL*Plus software allows calculations to be performed on the output derived from the execution of a Select command for its display format to be altered.

The Compute and Break commands allow calculations to be performed on the values displayed under a column. The things that can be Computed are the the sum and average of all values in a numeric column, the count of all occurrences under a column, the minimum and maximum values in a column, and the standard deviation and variance of values in a column.

For instance, consider the following SQL command:

```
Select Orderno,OrderLines.Stockno,Sname,Amount,
2    SPrice,SPrice*Amount
3    from OrderLines,Stock
4    where OrderLines.Stockno = Stock.Stockno
5    order by Orderno;
```

This command will find the names and prices of all items in the OrderLines relation and the cost of each item ordered. Thus for each line item in the OrderLines relation, its name and price must be retrieved from the Stock relation, and then its amount must be multiplied by its price to find its cost. Note on the last line, we have used the SQL clause order by to ensure that the output is displayed in Orderno order. This is important if calculations based on items that have a common Orderno are going to be carried out. Based on the sample database used in Chapter 3 the output given in Table 4.1 will result from this command.

This command by itself shows us the name and cost of each item order placed in the OrderLines file. There is a lot more information that would be useful and which could be extracted from this table. For instance, to know the total cost of each order might be helpful, as would a count of the number of different items placed in each order. Because

Table 4.1   Unformatted processing of OrderLines.

ORDERNO	STOCKNO	SNAME	AMOUNT	SPRICE	AMOUNT*SPRICE
1	1	Bolts	55	.15	8.25
1	3	Nails	124	.65	80.60
2	1	Bolts	24	.15	3.60
2	2	Nuts	35	.75	26.25
2	3	Nails	12	.65	7.80
2	4	Spanners	125	4.76	595.00
2	5	Screws	33	.11	3.63
3	1	Bolts	45	.15	6.75
3	2	Nuts	12	.75	9.00
3	3	Nails	234	.65	152.10
3	4	Spanners	13	4.76	61.88
3	3	Screws	145	.11	15.95
4	4	Spanners	32	4.76	152.32
4	5	Screws	125	.11	13.75

the output is in OrderNo order, it is quite easy to achieve these sorts of calculation.

First of all, we have to tell the system that we wish to perform a calculation each time the Orderno in the output changes. This is achieved by the SQL*Plus command:

Break on OrderNo

This has two effects. First of all, the system will now only print the value of Orderno when it changes. Also, it provides a checkpoint that can be used for performing calculations. What we want to do is to calculate the sum of all the values in the Amount*SPrice column each time the Orderno changes. This will give us the total cost of each order. We also wish to count the number of StockNo occurrences each time Orderno changes, giving us the number of different items on each order. This will be achieved by the commands:

Compute Sum Of Amount*SPrice On Orderno

Compute Count Of StockNo On OrderNo

Once these commands have been carried out, the output shown in Table 4.2 will be produced.

A count displayed is now under the StockNo column every time the OrderNo value changes and a Sum under the Amount*SPrice

Table 4.2 Use of SQL*Plus Aggregate Computations.

ORDERNO	STOCKNO	SNAME	AMOUNT	SPRICE	AMOUNT*SPRICE
1	1	Bolts	55	.15	8.25
	3	Nails	124	.65	80.6
**********	--------				----------------
count		2			
sum					88.85
2	1	Bolts	24	.15	3.6
	2	Nuts	35	.75	26.25
	3	Nails	12	.65	7.8
	4	Spanners	125	4.76	595
	5	Screws	33	.11	3.63
**********	--------				----------------
count		5			
sum					636.28
3	1	Bolts	45	.15	6.75
	2	Nuts	12	.75	9
	3	Nails	234	.65	152.1
	4	Spanners	13	4.76	61.88
	5	Screws	145	.11	15.95
**********	--------				----------------
count		5			
sum					245.68
4	4	Spanners	32	4.76	152.32
	5	Screws	125	.11	13.75
**********	--------				----------------
count		2			
sum					166.07

column. The output is not very easy to read in this respect as there are no spaces between the totals and the next values in the respective columns. This can be amended by changing the Break command.

> Break On OrderNo Skip 2

will cause two lines to be fed after each Break on OrderNo. The line feeds will occur after any summary totals are displayed, thus separating the summary information from the data in the columns. To display summary information at the end of the output, Compute and Break operations can be performed on Report. Suppose we wanted to have a total of the costs of all the Order items and an average of the cost of all the Order items. We would first have to amend the Break command thus:

Break On Report On OrderNo Skip 2

We would now have to add an extra Compute command:

Compute Avg Sum Of Amount*SPrice On Report

Running the SQL command above would give the same output as before except that there would now be two blank lines after the summary information for each OrderNo and at the end of the output under the Amount*SPrice column the values:

81.2057143
1136.88

would appear indicating the average cost of each order and the total cost of all the orders.

Note that the Break command had to be amended whereas we only had to add an extra Compute command. The system will only hold one Break command at a time: any new Break command will over-write the old one. If the command:

Break On Report

had been entered the summary information for each OrderNo would have been lost. The Compute command will only summarize those columns on which there is an active Break. Even though a Compute may not have been activated by a particular command, it is still resident in the system until it has been explicitly erased. This means that summary information can inadvertently appear in a given output because the user has managed to activate a dormant Compute. The command Computes will display all those Computes that are currently active. Clear Computes will erase all Computes from the system. Likewise, the command Breaks displays the currently active Breaks and Clear Breaks erases them. Clear Breaks will indirectly disable all Computes without actually erasing them.

The output is still not as readable as it might be. The numeric columns in particular are not in a particularly desirable format. SQL*Plus software contains a Col command which allows the format and headings of columns to be modified. For instance, if the OrderNo column were to be restricted to six figures with the heading OrderNo at the top, we would say:

Column OrderNo Format 999999 Heading 'OrderNo'

To amend the output of the Amount*SPrice column to something more acceptable, we could say:

Col Amount*SPrice Format 9999.99 Heading 'Cost'

In the above commands, the Format part specifies the width of the column by the number of 9 characters that follow it. The 9 character is used when the columns in question are numeric. Defining the width of a column for output is extremely useful as output which has a line width of more than 80 characters causes overflow resulting in unhelpful linefeeds being inserted which can render the final output very difficult to read. In the second command above, a decimal point was inserted. This means that all data displayed under this column will now consist of four numbers, followed by a decimal point, followed by two further numbers. This sort of specification is necessary to align numeric columns that are likely to have a large amount of decimal content, such as the Amount*SPrice column. Also in the second command, we have used the Col abbreviation for Column.

To re-specify the output format of a non-numeric column, the A character is used to specify its width. The following command

Col SName Format A10 Heading 'Item Name'

sets the width of SName to 10 characters and changes its heading to Item Name.

The Col command only affects the output appearance of a column; it has no effect on its underlying definition. It is not necessary to specify both the heading and the format of a column with Col because these are both optional clauses. As with Compute, any Col definitions are resident until the user ends their session using their Oracle software unless they are explicitly cleared. When entered by itself, Col will display all current column definitions. Clear Columns will erase them. Individual column definitions can be temporarily disabled. For instance, the command Col SName Off will disable the column definition for SName given above. Its display will revert to the default given by its Create Table definition. Col SName On will re-activate the tailored Col definition.

Col, Compute and Break commands are resident during a session until they have been explicitly erased and can give rise to unexpected output so, whenever they are put into a command file, it is good practice to Clear them at the end of the file.

Suppose it was necessary to formulate a command file that found all orders placed by the Leeds customers. For each order, the name of the customer is displayed along with the names of all items ordered, the cost of each item and the total value of the order. At the end the value of all the Leeds orders is to be listed. This data is to be output to the printer which has a page length of 65 lines with 5 lines of space between each page. The following commands will achieve this:

```
Set Buffer B
Input
1  Col OrderNo Format 999999 Heading 'OrderNo'
2  Col CustName Format A10 Heading 'Customer'
3  Col SName Format A10 Heading 'Item Name'
4  Col Amount*SPrice Format 9999.99 Heading 'Cost'
5  Break On OrderNo Skip 2 On Report
6  Compute Sum Of Amount*SPrice On OrderNo
7  Compute Sum Of Amount*SPrice On Report
8  Set PageSize 60
9  Set NewPage 5
10 Spool OrderSummaries
11 Select Orders.OrderNo,CustName,SName,Amount*Price
12 from Customers,Orders,OrderLines,Stock
13 where Stock.StockNo = OrderLines.StockNo
14         and OrderLines.OrderNo = Orders.OrderNo
15         and Orders.CustNo = Customers.CustNo
16         and Address = 'Leeds'
17 order by Orders.OrderNo;
18 Spool Out
19 Clear Breaks
20 Clear Computes
21 Clear Columns
Save OrderSummary
Start OrderSummary
```

This command file can now be called at any time and send the approprate information to the printer, leaving a copy of it in a host system file called OrderSummaries.lst. The Clear commands at the end mean that a no dormant Break, Col or Compute definitions are left active during the current Oracle user's session.

From this command our sample database will give the output shown in Table 4.3.

Titles can be placed at the beginning and end of this report with the SQL*Plus commands TTitle and BTitle. For instance, the commands:

```
TTitle Center 'Analysis of Leeds Orders'

BTitle Left 'Total of all Order Costs'
```

will cause the first message, the *header*, to be displayed at the head of each page of output and the latter, the *footer*, one to be displayed at the end of each page of output. The header will be printed in the centre of each page, whereas the footer will be printed at the left. Like Col, Break

Table 4.3   SQL*PLUS formatted report.

Orderno	Customer	Item Name	Cost
1	P. Jones	Bolts	8.25
		Nails	80.60
********			------
sum			88.85
2	P. Jones	Bolts	3.60
		Nuts	26.25
		Nails	7.80
		Spanners	595.00
		Screws	3.63
********			------
sum			636.28
4	B. Smith	Spanners	152.32
		Screws	13.75
********			------
sum			166.07

			891.20

and Compute, Title definitions remain in the system until explicitly cleared. The commands BTitle Off and TTitle Off achieve this.

To obtain summary information at the end of each page of output as well as at the end of the report, Breaks and Computes on Page can be set. The other Compute options available are Maximum, Minimum, Number, Std (standard deviation) and Variance.

At present, this report will only work for Leeds customers. If we wanted it to process our Colombo customers, we would have to change line 16 from 'Leeds' to 'Colombo', and likewise for any other address. It is possible using the SQL*Plus software to make this report more general using a parameter which can be entered when the command is activated with the Start command. If line 16 was changed to

and Address = '&City'

when the command Start OrderSummary is given, Oracle will return the following message:

Enter value for City :

The user can then enter any value for the address and the Oracle software will attempt to execute the command on this basis. Parameters can also be entered with the Start command. For instance,

Start OrderSummary 'Colombo'

will substitute the value Colombo into the first line where the & sign occurs.

This chapter has only outlined some of the summarizing and formatting options available as part of the SQL*Plus software. The SQL*Plus reference guide supplied with any Oracle implementation gives full details of the options available with the commands described herein. The software provides some basic and easy to use report-generation facilities. More advanced capabilities are provided by the SQL*Report module described in later chapters.

Key points

- In addition to the standard SQL commands common to all SQL-based systems, the manufacturers of the Oracle DBMS provide a number of extra commands to increase the functionality and usability of an Oracle system. This enhanced programming environment is called SQL*Plus.

- The SQL*Plus Set command allows the user to customize their environment.

- The SQL*Plus software provides a number of commands that enable the editing, storage, retrieval and execution of SQL*Plus command files.

- Direct calls to be made to the host computer's operating system are allowed by the SQL*Plus software.

- Simple reports can be generated by the SQL*Plus system using the Compute and Break commands to process data and the Col, TTitle and BTitle commands to format output.

- SQL*Plus command files can contain parameter values which only need to be entered at run-time.

EXERCISES

4.1 Write a command file consisting of SQL and SQL*Plus statements that will generate a printed report on the value of stock held in the database. The report should have the following headings:

Value of Stock Held

Stockno   Item Name   Unit Price   Level   Value

The report will contain one line for each item held in stock. The ItemName and Unit Price columns are derived from the SName and SPrice columns in the Stock table respectively. The Value column is derived from multiplying the SPrice of each item by its SLevel. A total reflecting the total value of all stock held should be at the foot of the report.

4.2 Write a command file containing SQL and SQL*Plus statements that generates a report indicating the total value of orders placed by city. The report will have the following headings:

City   OrderNo   StockNo   Value

and will contain one line per OrderLine placed. The value of each OrderLine is calculated by multiplying its Amount by its corresponding Sprice in the Stock table. The City column is derived from the Address column in the Customers table. The output must be in city order and after all the OrderLines placed against each city, there should be sub-totals indicating the total and average value of all OrderLines from that particular city. There should be a page break after each city and a summary at the end of the report indicating the total and average value of all OrderLines placed.

Five
A Brief Introduction to SQL*Forms

5.1 Designing a form
5.2 Operating a form
5.3 Re-defining function keys

Key points
Exercise

Most users of live database systems are not programmers. Although SQL is a simple language to learn compared with many other high-level languages used for data processing, it is both unrealistic and unreasonable to expect the average database user to be competent in the use of SQL before they are allowed to access and update the information held in an Oracle database.

The Oracle tool SQL*Forms has been built specifically to enable the construction of forms-based interfaces to the system, whereby the non-programming user can insert, update, delete and query the data held in a system by entering values on forms rather than by giving SQL commands. For instance, rather than giving the command:

    Select * from Customers
    where Address = 'Leeds';

to find records for all Leeds customers, it is possible to create a form over the Customers table which when activated initially consists of a series of blank columns as indicated in Figure 5.1.

Entering a value under any of these columns will then cause the system to display all those rows that it can find that contain that value.

81

```
┌─────────────────────────────────────────────────────────────────┐
│                  ======== CUSTOMERS ========                      │
│                                                                   │
│                                                                   │
│    CUSTNO      CUSTNAME              ADDRESS                       │
│    ──────      ────────              ───────────────────────────  │
│    ──────      ────────              ───────────────────────────  │
│    ──────      ────────              ───────────────────────────  │
│    ──────      ────────              ───────────────────────────  │
│    ──────      ────────              ───────────────────────────  │
└─────────────────────────────────────────────────────────────────┘
```

Figure 5.1   A default form for the Customers table.

Thus entering the word Leeds under the Address column will result in the displaying of all rows in the Customers table whose address is Leeds. Combinations of values can also be searched for. Entering the value Leeds under Address and >'M' under Custname will restrict the display to just those Leeds customers whose name starts with a letter in the second half of the alphabet. This sort of querying is known as *query by example,* and most leading relational products provide such an interface to their systems.

Forms created in SQL*Forms also allow the data within tables to be updated, deleted and inserted directly from the forms themselves. Even for a skilled SQL programmer, deleting and updating single records through a form is often quicker and easier than entering the appropriate SQL command. Creating new records through a form is invariably less time-consuming than using endless SQL Insert commands.

There are essentially two modes in which SQL*Forms is used: the *designer's mode* and the *operator's mode.* The designer defines a form in terms of its appearance and the tables that it is built over. The operator uses the form in order to interrogate and manipulate the data in the underlying database. This chapter is therefore split into two sections: *designing* a form and *operating* a form.

In either mode, SQL*Forms makes use of a number of predefined functions that are activated by the user pressing the appropriate keys on the computer keyboard. The range of functions are the same on every machine. What does vary are the key combinations necessary to activate them. An SQL*Forms function here will be indicated by use of the < . . . > brackets. For instance, in both modes, there is a <select> function to activate a choice off a menu. The key depression necessary to enable <select> is detailed in the Oracle SQL*Forms manual for a given machine. Additionally, on all versions of SQL*Forms, there is a <help> key, which, when depressed, displays the key depressions necessary to

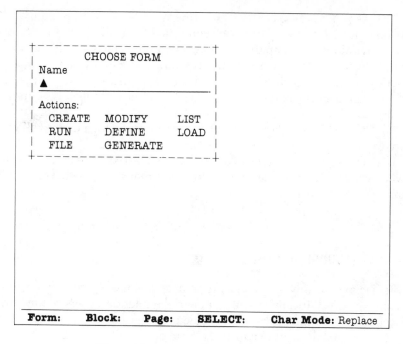

```
+--------------------+
|      CHOOSE FORM   |
| Name               |
| ▲                  |
|_____|
| Actions:           |
|  CREATE   MODIFY    LIST  |
|  RUN      DEFINE    LOAD  |
|  FILE     GENERATE        |
+--------------------+
```

Form: Block: Page: **SELECT:**   **Char Mode:** Replace

Figure 5.2   The Choose Form window.

activate all the other available functions. <help> can be activated at any time in SQL*Forms.

SQL*Forms itself makes extensive use of windows. A window typically has a heading, a fill-in part and a list of actions. For instance, when you first invoke SQL*Forms from the host computer, the Oracle software displays the login window. On this, you are required to enter your Oracle account name and password and then press the <accept> button. This takes you to the Choose Form window shown in Figure 5.2.

At this point the name of the form to be used must be entered and the desired action <select>ed. To <select> an action, the carriage return key is depressed and the system takes the cursor from one action to the next. Once the cursor is positioned next to the required action, the <select> button must then be depressed. According to the selected action, another window may appear requiring more data to be entered and a further action to be selected or a form itself may be displayed. To return from one window to the previous one, the <exit/cancel> button may be depressed. There are many instances when it is appropriate to use the <accept> button to save the work that has been done in a particular window before returning to the previous one.

As well as these Action-type windows, there are other types such as List and Switch windows. Selecting the List action from the Choose Form window brings up the List Form window which lists all the forms currently available to an account. A Switch-type window lists characteristics that may be switched on or off for the particular object on which the designer is currently working. These will be described later in this chapter.

The actions selected on the Choose Form window will vary according to whether one is operating or designing a form. In either mode, there is a great range of options available to the user. This chapter will concentrate on those options that will be used most frequently in the design and use of forms.

5.1   Designing a form

The designer of any form needs to understand the use to which a form will be put and, ideally, a knowledge of the intended users of the form. Designers of Oracle forms will also need to have a detailed knowledge of the Oracle database over which the form is going to be built. A form in SQL*Forms can only be built over tables and views that have been explicitly Created in SQL*Plus. SQL*Forms cannot be used to initially define a table.

5.1.1   Basic forms concepts

● *Blocks*

A form in SQL*Forms is composed of one or more *blocks*. A block contains records composed of fields. The data in these fields and records is derived from an underlying table or view held in an Oracle database. By default, each record corresponds to a row from the underlying table or view, and each field corresponds to a column from the underlying table or view. Although a screen may contain a number of blocks, each block is physically distinct so data entered in one block has no effect on the data displayed in another. It is possible, however, to cross-relate the data between blocks automatically by means of user-defined triggers.

● *Triggers*

A *trigger* is an action or set of actions that the form designer can specify to happen when a certain event occurs or key is struck. As well as cross-relating data between blocks, triggers can be used to validate input, process and amend the data displayed in a form, enforce security checks and so on. Some simple examples of triggers will be given in this text.

5.1.2 Creating a default form

When creating a form, the form and the blocks that it is comprised of must each be named, the table or view over which each block is built must be identified and finally the form has to be saved. When using the default options in form design, the widths and names of the displayed items in the form follow the specification used in the relevant SQL Create commands for the underlying tables and views.

This section will describe how to create a form built over two blocks. The name of the form will be OrderForm and the blocks will be called Heading and Details. The Heading block will be built over the Orders table and the Details block over the OrderLines table. The idea is to have a form at the head of which will be the order number, customer number and order date. Underneath there will be a list of up to 10 stock numbers and their corresponding amounts placed on the order. By using the default options, the form will appear as in Figure 5.3.

This is, of course, not the most attractive of display formats. Neither does it contain all the information the user will need – the names and addresses of the customers should appear as well as the names and prices of each stock item. Fortunately, it is possible to modify a default form considerably in appearance and in the amount of information it displays once it has been created.

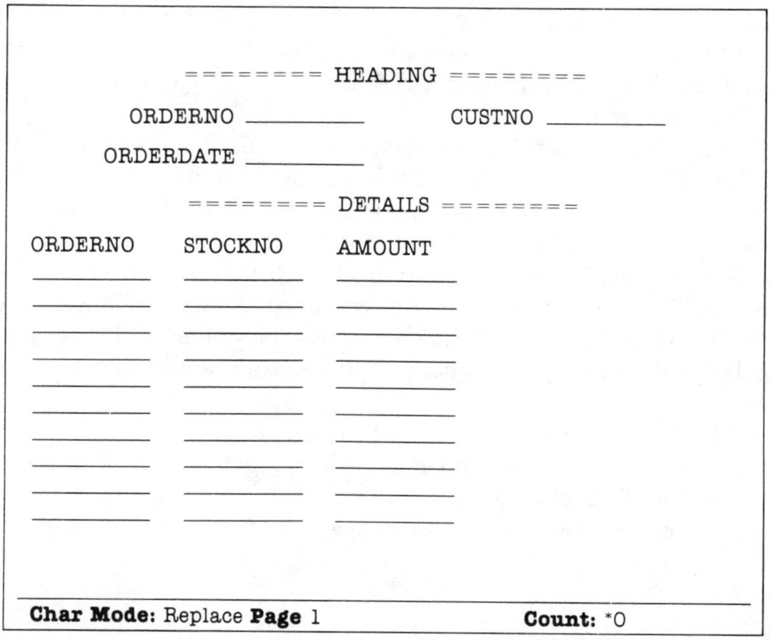

Figure 5.3 A default OrderForm.

To create a default form, one must first enter a name for the form in the Choose Form window as shown in Figure 5.4.

Next, it is necessary to position the cursor next to Create and <select> this action. This will bring up the Choose Block window. Note how each window activated in the Design mode overlays the previous one. For convenience, however, this will often be implied rather than explicitly drawn in this text.

The first block is to be called Heading, thus Heading must be entered next to the Name of the block. It is now necessary to move the cursor down to Default. All this is shown in Figure 5.5. When the <select> button is depressed, the Default Block window appears, as in Figure 5.6.

It is now that the underlying table or view over which the block is built is specified. Next to Name, the name of a table or view must be entered. If it is not accessible to the Oracle account where the form is being designed, an error message will be displayed. By moving to the Tables action and pressing <select>, a list of the available tables will be displayed as in Figure 5.7. By placing the cursor next to a member of this list and pressing <select> followed by <accept>, the name of this table will be automatically entered next to the Name of the default block.

Rows Displayed indicates how many rows from a table may be displayed on the screen at once. The default is one, but this can be increased to any number of rows *whose width is less than 80 characters.*

Thus, for the Heading block, Orders should be entered in the space for the Table Name in the Default Block window and the Rows Displayed should be left unchanged as there is only one header record per order placed.

Pressing <accept> at this stage will return control to the Choose Block window. Now the word Details should be placed against Name and Default <select>ed again. This time, OrderLines should be entered against the Table Name and the Rows Displayed changed to 10. Pressing <accept> once will return control to the Choose Block window. Pressing <accept> twice will return control to Choose Form. In this window, the action FILE should now be <select>ed – see Figure 5.8. This will bring up a number of options, from which Save should be <select>ed.

The system will now have a definition of the form described above which may be Generated and Run to interrogate and update the data held in the OrderLines and Orders tables. However, before the operation of this form is examined, we will Modify it to make it more useful.

5.1.3   Altering a form

As in its creation, a form is Modifyed by changing the definitions of the blocks that it comprises. Currently, our form OrderForm is made up of

```
┬ ─ ─ ─ ─ ─ ─ ─ ─ ─ ─ ─ ─ ─ ─ ─ ┬
│          CHOOSE FORM           │
│ Name                           │
│ OrderForm _____  │
│ Actions:                       │
│ ▲CREATE    MODIFY     LIST     │
│   RUN      DEFINE     LOAD      │
│   FILE     GENERATE            │
┴ ─ ─ ─ ─ ─ ─ ─ ─ ─ ─ ─ ─ ─ ─ ─ ┴
```

Form: **Block:**   **Page:**   **SELECT:**   **Char Mode:** Replace

Figure 5.4 Specifying the creation of OrderForm.

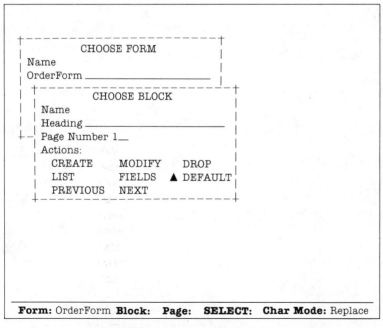

Form: OrderForm **Block:**   **Page:**   **SELECT:**   **Char Mode:** Replace

Figure 5.5 Specifying the Default creation of the Heading block.

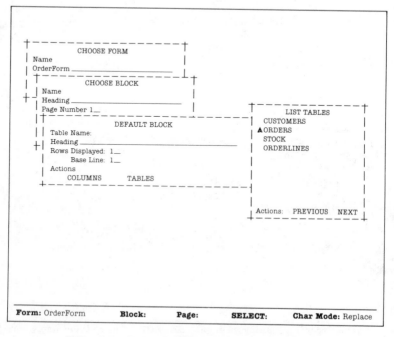

Figure 5.6　The Default Block window.

Figure 5.7　Activating the List Tables window.

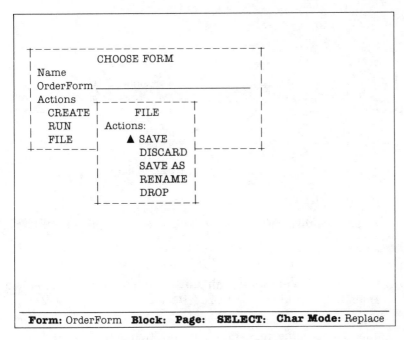

Figure 5.8 The File window.

two blocks built over the tables OrderLines and Orders respectively. The Heading block built over Orders looks something like Figure 5.9.

It would be desirable to change its appearance and also to incorporate some more information, such as the name and address of the customer, the value of the order, and the name of the firm sending the order, resulting in a block looking like that shown in Figure 5.10.

Likewise, the Details block could be improved by moving some of the displayed fields around, changing their headings and incorporating the names and unit prices of the items ordered and the cost of each item ordered, resulting in a block like the one shown in Figure 5.11.

```
======= HEADING =======

    ORDERNO _____        CUSTNO _____

    ORDERDATE _____
```

Figure 5.9 Default heading block display.

```
                    Speedy Deliveries Ltd

Order No   ____________        Customer Name  ____________
Customer   ____________        Address        ____________
Date       ____________        Cost of Order  ____________
```

Figure 5.10 Modified **Heading** block.

To achieve this, the following tasks need to be performed:

1. Amend the definition of the table Orders to include a column specifying the total cost of each order,
2. Re-create a default form with a heading block built over the amended definition of the Orders table,
3. Use the *Screen Painter* to enable new fields to appear on the form and to amend the appearance and position of the current fields of data,
4. Write a Trigger that causes the name and address of a Customer to be displayed in the Heading block every time a customer number is entered into this block,
5. Write a Trigger that extracts the name and price of an item from the Stock table every time its stock number value is entered onto the Details block,
6. Write Triggers that calculate the cost of each item ordered and also the total cost of the order each time an amount value is entered onto the Details block,
7. Specify that records in the Details block are restricted to only those OrderLines which relate to the record displayed in the Heading block.

It is not necessary (or even always desirable) to perform all of these steps before using the form. The simple queries outlined in the section on operating a form can be performed on the form at any stage of its development, including the default stage. In fact, it is desirable to test the operation of the form at every stage of its development. If the form is not tested until the end of the design stage and there have been errors made in its design, then it is very hard to determine where these errors actually occur. However, if the form is tested after each amendment,

```
┌─────────────────────────────────────────────────────────────────┐
│                          Items Ordered                            │
│                                                                   │
│                                                                   │
│  Order No  Stock No   Description      Amount   Unit Price   Cost │
│  _____  _____  _____    _____  _____  _____ │
│  _____  _____  _____    _____  _____  _____ │
│  _____  _____  _____    _____  _____  _____ │
│  _____  _____  _____    _____  _____  _____ │
│  _____  _____  _____    _____  _____  _____ │
│  _____  _____  _____    _____  _____  _____ │
│  _____  _____  _____    _____  _____  _____ │
│  _____  _____  _____    _____  _____  _____ │
│  _____  _____  _____    _____  _____  _____ │
│  _____  _____  _____    _____  _____  _____ │
│                                                                   │
│                                                                   │
│                                                                   │
│                                                                   │
│ Char Mode: Replace        Page: 1            Count: *0            │
└─────────────────────────────────────────────────────────────────┘
```

Figure 5.11   Modified Details block.

whenever it fails to function, the most likely cause of failure will be the most recent amendment.

That said, each of the above steps can now be looked at in detail.

5.1.3.1   *Amending the definition of orders*

This cannot be done within SQL*Forms. Instead, the user will have to exit from SQL*Forms and enter SQL*PLus and use the appropriate Alter Table command

```
Alter Table Orders
2    Add OrderCost Number;
```

5.1.3.2   *Re-creating the default form*

From the Choose Form window, the form OrderForm should be specified and the action File <selected>ed. From the file options listed, the Drop option should be chosen. This removes the former definition for OrderForm from the system. This is necessary if the underlying tables that support a form have had their definitions changed and the user wishes the form to reflect these changes.

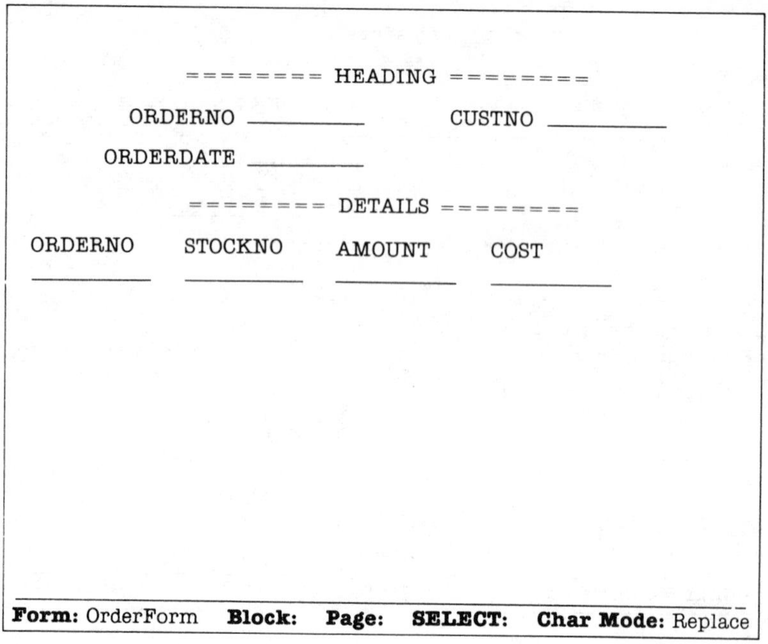

```
========= HEADING =========

        ORDERNO _____          CUSTNO _____

      ORDERDATE _____


        ========= DETAILS =========

 ORDERNO      STOCKNO      AMOUNT         COST

 _____  _____  _____    _____
```

Form: OrderForm   **Block:**   **Page:**   **SELECT:**   **Char Mode:** Replace

Figure 5.12   Screen Painter display of default blocks.

An alternative to Dropping the former default definition is to use the Save As option from the File options. This effectively renames the form.

Whichever course of action is followed, a new default version of OrderForm may now be Created by entering its name in the Choose Form window and following the steps described in 5.1.2 above.

5.1.3.3 *Using the Screen Painter to position and define fields*
The Screen Painter can be used for changing the appearance of a form in a number of ways. The actual fields displayed can be altered as well as their positions on the screen. The widths of the fields can be amended as can the format of the data that they display. Many other columns of the fields including their associated Triggers, which will be described below, are also determined from the Screen Painter.

To access the Screen Painter, the designer enters the name of the form to be amended on the Choose Form window and <select>s the Modify action. This brings up the Choose Block window. Here, the name of the block to be amended must be entered and the Modify action <select>ed. This will display the form in its current state, ready for amending – see Figure 5.12.

```
┌─────────────────────────────────────────────────────────────┐
│                                                               │
│                    Speedy Deliveries Ltd                      │
│                                                               │
│                                                               │
│      Order No  _____      Customer Name               │
│      Customer  _____      Address                     │
│      Date      _____      Cost of Order               │
│                                                               │
│                                                               │
└─────────────────────────────────────────────────────────────┘
```

Figure 5.13   The amended Heading block.

To change the text displayed in a block, move the cursor to where the new text is to be and type in the desired text. All the default headings can be amended quite simply by typing over them with something more desirable. For instance, to modify the title of the Heading block, the designer simply moves the cursor to the Heading title and over-types it with the new heading.

For changing the position of a field, SQL*Forms provides <cut> and <paste> actions. To use this facility, the designer must first move the cursor to the start of the field to be moved and press <cut>. The cursor is then moved to where the designer wants the field to be and <paste> pressed. This will move the data space for the field, but not its heading. Thus, after using <cut> and <paste>, it is usually necessary to re-enter text on the form. Therefore, when amending a form, it is normally better to perform all the required <cut> and <paste> actions first and to amend the text afterwards. If an action other than <paste> is specified after a <cut>, the field is removed from the form altogether. This can be retrieved by the <undo> action. This will delete the last action performed in a block and can be used repeatedly to delete a whole series of actions.

The default fields displayed on each block can be moved about at will by using <cut> and <paste> and text can be altered or entered as appropriate. New field can be entered on a block using the <create field> function. Suppose that after the initial <cut> and <paste> a heading block that looked like the one shown in Figure 5.13.

As this stands, there are no spaces as yet for customers names and addresses. This is because they are fields based on columns that do not exist in the Orders table over which the block is built. To insert a field on a form, it is necessary to perform the following steps:

1.   Move the cursor to the desired starting position of the field. In the first instance, this will be two spaces after the phrase Customer Name. Press the button <select>.

2.   Press the <right arrow> as many times as the desired display width of the field. For instance, for a ten character field, <right arrow> should be pressed ten times. Press <select> again. These two actions establish the position and width of the field on the form.

3.   Press the <create field> button. This brings up the Define Field window which is used to specify a field definition (Figure 5.14).

A field is defined in terms of its name, data type and any actions to be taken on it. For the Customer Name field, it is necessary to enter a name (e.g. CustName) next to Name on the Define Field window. The default data type for all fields is Char. This will not need to be amended for the CustName field. To change the data type, the cursor has to be moved next to the desired type and <select> pressed. It is worth noting here that there are a lot more data types available in SQL*Forms than in SQL*Plus. The specification of a data type for a field in SQL*Forms does not affect its underlying SQL*Plus definition, it simply alters the way it is displayed on the form. Of course, it is necessary to ensure that the data type selected in SQL*Forms is compatible with its underlying definition.

The actions to be taken on a field are optional. The Trigger action

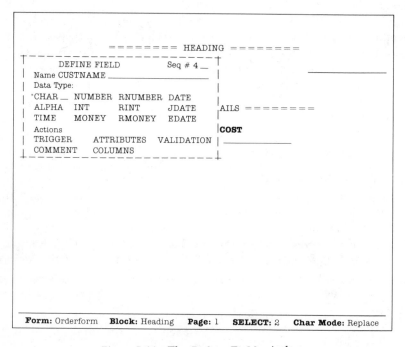

Figure 5.14   The Define Field window.

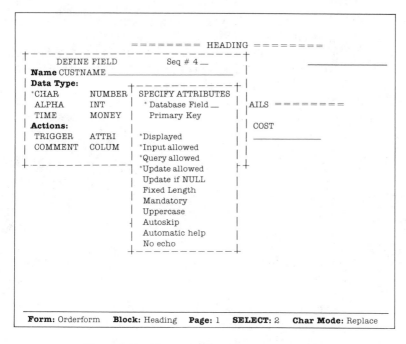

```
               ======== HEADING ========
+ - - - - - - - - - - - - - - - - - - - - - +
|    DEFINE FIELD          Seq # 4 __        |              _____
| Name CUSTNAME _____                        |
| Data Type:          + - - - - - - - - - - +  |
| *CHAR      NUMBER | SPECIFY ATTRIBUTES  | |
|  ALPHA     INT    | * Database Field __  | |AILS ========
|  TIME      MONEY  |   Primary Key        | |
| Actions:          |                      | | COST
|  TRIGGER   ATTRI  |                      | | _____
|  COMMENT   COLUM  | *Displayed           | |
+ - - - - - - - - - |*Input allowed        | |
                    | *Query allowed       | |
                    | *Update allowed      | +
                    |  Update if NULL      |
                    |  Fixed Length        |
                    |  Mandatory           |
                    |  Uppercase           |
                    |  Autoskip            |
                    |  Automatic help      |
                    |  No echo             |
                    + - - - - - - - - - - +

Form: Orderform   Block: Heading   Page: 1   SELECT: 2   Char Mode: Replace
```

Figure 5.15 The Specify Attributes window.

specifies events that may be triggered off by a field. Triggers will be discussed with examples later on. Validation allows criteria to be specified that check the validity of a field when a value is entered for it on the screen. Columns displays the names of the columns in the table over which a block is built. Attributes enables certain characteristics of the field to be set.

With our field, CustName, it is necessary to alter some of the default attributes. To do this, it is necessary to move the cursor to the Attributes action and press <select>. This brings up the Specify Attributes window which is shown in Figure 5.15. This window lists a number of 'switches' which may be set on or off for a particular field. The * indicates those switches that are on. In Figure 5.15 certain attributes are assigned by default to all fields initially. The Database Field switch indicates that the data values for the field are extracted from the base table over which the block is built. This is not true for CustName. This switch must therefore be de-selected. To do this, the cursor must be placed next to it and <select> pressed. The * disappears, indicating that it is no longer active. On this form, it would be desirable to de-select Input allowed and Query allowed on the CustName field as this information is not held in the tables over which the block is built. When Input Allowed is de-selected, the attribute

Update allowed is automatically de-selected. <select> is also used to activate a non-active switch.

Having changed the attributes as necessary, <accept> must then be pressed. This returns the user to the Define Field window. Pressing <accept> again returns the user to the Screen Painter, which will now have a data space assigned to the new field.

The above steps can now be repeated for the Address field. This should now leave the heading block looking like the one shown in Figure 5.10.

Oracle provides an optional form of entity integrity through SQL*Forms. This can be achieved by following these steps: Before leaving the heading block, to move the cursor to the OrderNo field and press <define>. This will bring up the Define Field window described above. Then <select> the Attributes action and from there <select> the Primary Key column, as OrderNo is the primary key for the underlying table. Once this is done, the Oracle software will prevent an order being created from the screen that does not have an order number, and will also ensure that these are unique.

The Screen Painter can only work on one block at a time. Thus, when the Header block is complete, the <accept> button must be pressed to commit these changes to the screen definition. This returns the user to the Choose Block window, where the Details block must now be named and the Modify action <select>ed to enable the movement and re-labelling of existing fields in that block and the positioning, labelling and initial definition of the new fields Description, UnitPrice and Cost depicted in Figure 5.16.

5.1.3.4 *Writing* Triggers *for the* Heading *block*

When a field is defined, any number of Triggers may be linked to it. As the name suggests, a value in one field can be used to trigger off a host of actions that effect the values in other fields. In the previous section, entering two new fields (CustName and Address) onto the Heading block was described. They were defined as *non-database fields*, that is, their values could not be extracted from the table over which the block was built. Instead, they have to be extracted from another table, the Customers table. To do this, a Trigger has to be set on the CustNo in the Heading block to perform a join between the CustNo on the form and the CustNo column in the Customers table. To set a Trigger, it is necessary to access the Screen Painter for a block as described above. Once in the Screen Painter, the cursor must be moved to the desired field (in this case Customer Number) and the <define> button pressed. This brings up the Define Field window as described above. In this window, the designer must now <select> the action Trigger. This brings up the Choose Trigger window shown in Figure 5.17.

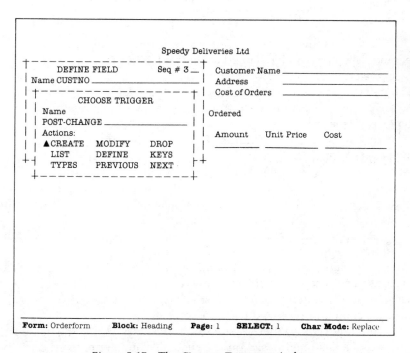

Speedy Deliveries Ltd

Order No _____   Customer Name _____
Customer _____   Address   _____
Date   _____   Cost of Order   _____

Items Ordered

Order No	StockNo	Description	Amount	Unit Price	Cost
_____	_____	_____	_____	_____	_____

Form: Orderform   **Block:** Details   **Page:** 1   **SELECT:**   **Char Mode:** Replace

Figure 5.16 OrderForm amended through Screen Painter.

Speedy Deliveries Ltd

```
+ - - - - - - - - - - - - - - - +
|    DEFINE FIELD      Seq # 3 _ |   Customer Name _____
| Name CUSTNO _____   |   Address       _____
| + - - - - - - - - - - - - - + |   Cost of Orders _____
| |     CHOOSE TRIGGER       | |
| | Name                     | |   Ordered
| | POST-CHANGE _____ | |
| | Actions:                 | |   Amount   Unit Price   Cost
| | ▲CREATE   MODIFY    DROP  | |   _____   _____   _____
+ | LIST     DEFINE    KEYS  | +
+ | TYPES    PREVIOUS  NEXT  | +
  + - - - - - - - - - - - - - +
```

Form: Orderform   **Block:** Heading   **Page:** 1   **SELECT:** 1   **Char Mode:** Replace

Figure 5.17 The Choose Trigger window.

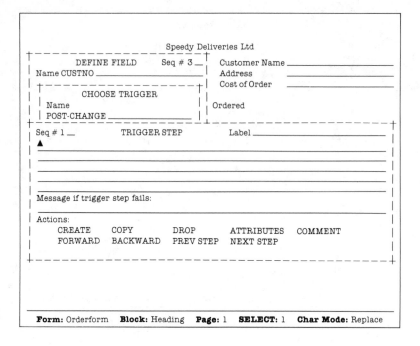

Figure 5.18   The Trigger Step window.

This window can be called up from various windows. This is because Triggers can be defined at the field, block or form level. In this case, we are defining a field-level Trigger. Depending on what level of Trigger you are writing, there is a range of available Trigger types. By <select>ing the action Types from the window, the range of available types is displayed.

In this case, a Post-Change Trigger is needed. This is one that is activated *after* a data value has been entered into a field, that is, when a customer number is entered, it then has to find the name and address relating to it. Thus, Post-Change should be entered into the Name for the Trigger, and the action Create <select>ed. This brings up the Trigger Step window as shown in Figure 5.18.

A Trigger is composed of a series of sequential steps. The sequence in which these steps is executed can be altered by over-writing the Seq # value in the top-left hand of the window. The actions Next Step and Prev Step allow the designer to examine each step defined in a Trigger and to amend them as desired. A step is created by using the Create action and removed by the Drop action.

For this Trigger, there is one step to execute: finding the name and address of a customer based on the customer number entered onto the form. To do this it is necessary to <select> the Create action and enter

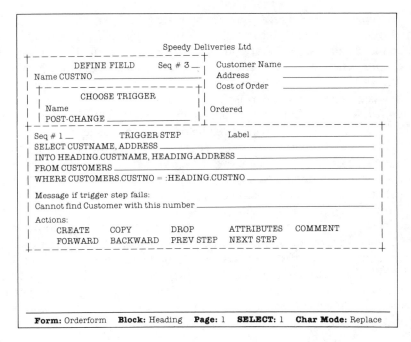

Figure 5.19 Entering a Trigger Step.

the text as indicated in Figure 5.19. This is a special variant of the SQL Select statement. The syntax has been extended to include references to blocks on the form as well as tables in the database.

The first line identifies the columns to be retrieved, as in the standard SQL Select statement. The second line specifies where on the form the Selected data is to be displayed, thus the requirement for the word Into followed by the names of those blocks and fields into which the data is to be put. It is not legal on this line to use the names of any tables or views in the underlying database. On the third line, From specifies where the data is to be found. In this case, it must be an underlying table or view that exists in the database. There is an exception to this. The table name Dual can be used when moving information from one part of the form to another. (See Section 5.1.3.6 for further discussion of Dual.) The Where part specifies the constraints on the Selection. On this line, the system is instructed to find the Customer row whose number matches the number entered on the Heading block. The use of the : before the word Heading indicates that Heading is a block, and *not an underlying table*. This resolves any possible ambiguities that may arise from statements that reference blocks and tables together. Note that the : is not required on the Into line as only blocks may be referenced on this line.

There is also an entry under Message if trigger step fails. This message will be displayed whilst the form is actually in use if the Select statement fails to yield any data. This special form of the Select statement also has a different effect to that which it has in SQL*Plus. Whereas in SQL*Plus, all those records that satisfy the query will be displayed, with an SQL*Forms Trigger, only the first record found will be returned. Thus, this feature is usually only of great use when, as in this instance, there should only be one record that satisfies the query. To display a set of records requires a slightly different mechanism, which will be described in 5.1.3.7 below.

Having defined a Trigger, <accept> must be pressed until the designer is back at the Choose Form window. Once this has been done, the form should be Filed, Generated and Run to test the execution of the Trigger. When creating a multi-step Trigger, it is best to do this after each step of the Trigger has been specified, because locating the exact source of an error in a Trigger of this type can be difficult once it is completed. After the initial Create, extra steps may be added to a Trigger by <select>ing the Modify action from the Choose Trigger window, followed by the appropriate Next Step, Prev Step, Drop and Create actions.

5.1.3.5   Triggers *in the* Details *block*

As in the Heading block, data needs to be found for the Details block that is derived from an underlying table over which the block has not been built. In this case, we wish to find the price and name of an item in the Details block based on the stock number entered for it. This can be done by Createing the following Trigger on the Stockno field in the Details block:

```
Select SName, SPrice
Into Details.ItemName, Details.ItemPrice
From Stock
Where Stock.StockNo = :Details.StockNo
```

As before, this Trigger should be tested before proceeding to the next step.

5.1.3.6   *Deriving logical information from the* Details *block*

The Triggers described above display data that is taken from an underlying table. It is possible to process this data for display on the form which can be written back to the database. For instance, data regarding the actual cost of each item ordered is not held in the database. However, there is enough information on the *form* to calculate this and display it. Each time an amount for an item is entered, it can be multiplied by its displayed price and the result entered under its cost. Thus, the following Post-Change Trigger step can be defined for the

Amount field in the Details block:

```
Select :ItemPrice * :Amount
Into Cost
From System.Dual
```

Use is made here of the dummy table Dual owned by the System account. Dual is is a special single-row, single-column table supplied by the system for the use of temporary variables. Each time an amount of goods is entered into the Details block, it will be multiplied by its corresponding price. The result is first written into Dual and from there to the corresponding cost value. Dual can only work on single row values – for example, it cannot be used for calculating aggregates. So, to find the total cost of all the items on an order and to display this result, a second step must be added to the Post-Change Trigger on Amount which consults the base tables:

```
Select Sum (SPrice * Amount)
Into Heading.OrderCost
From Stock, OrderLines, Orders
Where Stock.StockNo = OrderLines.StockNo
And OrderLines.OrderNo = Orders.OrderNo
And Orders.OrderNo = :Heading.OrderNo
```

This Trigger step uses the SQL Sum function to add up all the values in the specified columns that satisfy the given constraint. Here the system is being told that each time an amount is entered into the Details block, it is to calculate the total cost of all those items in the database that relate to the OrderNo in the Heading block, and display this total cost in the OrderCost field in the Heading block.

5.1.3.7   *Tieing together two blocks on a form*
We currently have two blocks on the form which can be queried quite independently of each other. When operating the form, it is possible to query records in the Details block which have nothing to do with the records displayed in the Heading block and vice versa. However, information now appears in the Heading block (the order cost) which relates to the Detail records displayed below. It is possible, however, to make the OrderNo in the Details block always be the same as the OrderNo in the Heading block. To do this, the form designer must access the Screen Painter for the Details block, move to the OrderNo field, press <define> to bring up the Define Field window and <select> the Validation action. This brings up the Specify Validation window depicted in Figure 5.20.

This window displays the default display lengths and help messages for a given field. If necessary, these may be amended by over-writing them in this window. Specification of the acceptable range of

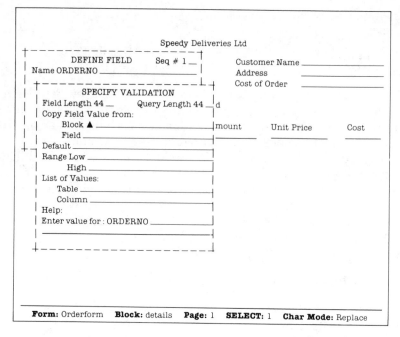

Figure 5.20   The Specify Validation window.

values for a field is also possible. There is additionally the facility to specify that a field takes its value from another field on the form. In this instance, entering Heading next to Block and OrderNo next to Field and pressing <accept> means that from now on, when a value is placed in the OrderNo field on the Heading block, when the cursor is moved to the Details block, the same OrderNo will appear automatically in the Details block OrderNo field. In this way, records displayed in the Details block may be restricted to only those OrderLines that 'belong' to the Order designated in the Heading block.

5.2   Operating a form

Once a form has been built in SQL*Forms, it may be used to query, insert, update and delete data in the underlying database. The range of operations allowable in a given form is constrained by two things:

1. The underlying database definition of the tables over which the form is built,

2. Any validation and column specifications built in by the form designer.

If the operator attempts to perform an action that is not allowed by the underlying database definition of the relevant tables, SQL*Forms simply informs them that an Oracle error has occurred. This is not a particularly helpful message, and can be quite disturbing for the average, non-programming forms user. To avoid error messages being displayed too often, the designer should make extensive use of the facilities provided by SQL*Forms to validate data entry and provide help messages before presenting the form as ready for use by the operator. In this section, ways in which some simple queries and updates can be performed in SQL*Forms shall be examined, along with guidelines on how to use it to enter data into a table.

5.2.1   Querying a form

In most environments, there are two ways to invoke a defined Oracle form:

1.   Directly from the operating system; or
2.   From within SQL*Forms.

To invoke a form from the operating system, the Runform command may be used. The format of this command is:

Runform form_name [username/password]

If the user name and password are not entered on the command line, the Oracle software prompts the user to supply these before it will retrieve, generate and run the form.

To invoke a form for operation from within the SQL*Forms software, on the other hand, its name must be entered into the Choose Form window and the Generate action selected. This causes the system to check that the form definition is valid: that it is built over tables that actually exist in the database and that the basic syntax of the triggers is correct. Once Generated, the Run action must be selected. This brings up the form for use as currently designed. The effects of the queries outlined below will vary according to the state of the form design in terms of the quantity of information displayed in each record in the respective blocks. The examples of output given below are based on the default version of the OrderForm.

SQL*Forms works on the *query by example* principle. The operator enters examples of the data to be selected, and the database attempts to find data that corresponds to these examples. When a form is displayed on the screen, the cursor is placed in the first field of the first block. The <next field> function moves the cursor from one field to the next within a block. The <next block> and <previous block> functions

```
┌──────────────────────────────────────────────────────────────┐
│                                                                │
│              ======== HEADING ========                        │
│                                                                │
│          ORDERNO 1_____          CUSTNO _____          │
│                                                                │
│        ORDERDATE _____                                     │
│                                                                │
│              ======== DETAILS ========                        │
│                                                                │
│    ORDERNO    STOCKNO    AMOUNT     COST                       │
│   _____  _____  _____  _____                   │
│   _____  _____  _____  _____                   │
│   _____  _____  _____  _____                   │
│   _____  _____  _____  _____                   │
│   _____  _____  _____  _____                   │
│   _____  _____  _____  _____                   │
│   _____  _____  _____  _____                   │
│   _____  _____  _____  _____                   │
│   _____  _____  _____  _____                   │
│                                                                │
│                                                                │
│ ──────────────────────────────────────────────────────────── │
│ Char Mode: Replace    Page: 1   ENTER QUERY   Count: *0        │
└──────────────────────────────────────────────────────────────┘
```

Figure 5.21   Entering a query on the Heading block.

move the cursor from one block to another. When a query is entered, it is activated in the context of the block where the cursor is. It has no effect on the display of data in other blocks unless the form designer has explicitly written triggers or validations that relate the data in one block to that in another.

To perform a query, the operator must press the <enter query> key. The Oracle software will then prompt the operator to enter the search parameters for the query. For instance, having loaded OrderForm, the operator may press the <enter query> key and enter the number 1 into the OrderNo space in the Heading block. This is shown in Figure 5.21. Having entered this search parameter, the operator may now press <execute query> and the system will find the row with this OrderNo value in the underlying table Orders and display it in the relevant fields in the Heading block as in Figure 5.22.

The diagram illustrates the effect of executing this query on the *default* version of OrderForm. Executing a query will also cause any triggers on the fields effected by the query to be activated. Thus, in the modified version of the form, the name and address of the Customer that matches the CustNo value now displayed will be retrieved and displayed in the Name and Address fields.

```
======== HEADING ========

     ORDERNO 1_____          CUSTNO 1_____

  ORDERDATE 24-JAN-86

       ======== DETAILS ========

ORDERNO      STOCKNO      AMOUNT      COST

_____     _____     _____    _____
_____     _____     _____    _____
_____     _____     _____    _____
_____     _____     _____    _____
_____     _____     _____    _____
_____     _____     _____    _____
_____     _____     _____    _____
_____     _____     _____    _____
_____     _____     _____    _____


Char Mode: Replace        Page: 1            Count: 1
```

Figure 5.22   Execution of a Query on the Heading block.

This is an example of a single record retrieval. If the number 1 had been entered in the Customer number field, the system would find more than one row that satisfied the query. However, the Heading block only displays a single record at a time. To overcome this sort of problem, SQL*Forms has the <next record> and <previous record> functions. Using these enables the operator to examine sets of records that are too big to fit onto the form as defined.

Forms can also be queried on more than one field in a block. For instance, in the Details block, one could execute a query by entering 1 under OrderNo and 1 under StockNo. The system will now retrieve those OrderLine records with an OrderNo of 1 *and* a StockNo of 1. A query can be performed on as many fields as are displayed in a block, except for those fields on which the attribute Query Allowed has been de-selected. The usual range of comparative operators can be used as well. Entering 1 under the OrderNo in the Details block and >100 under the Amount will display those records with an OrderNo of 1 and an Amount of greater than 100.

Records can also be queried on a range of values. If we wanted, for example, to find all the orders placed between two dates, we could

```
======== HEADING ========
    ORDERNO &DATE____        CUSTNO _____
    ORDERDATE _____

    ======== DETAILS ========
ORDERNO    STOCKNO    AMOUNT    COST
_____    _____    _____   _____
_____    _____    _____   _____
_____    _____    _____   _____
_____    _____    _____   _____
_____    _____    _____   _____
_____    _____    _____   _____
_____    _____    _____   _____
_____    _____    _____   _____
_____    _____    _____   _____

Query Where ... > &DATE between '01-FEB-86' and '28-FEB-86'
```

Figure 5.23   Querying the Heading block on a range value.

perform the following actions:

1.   Move the cursor to the Heading block;
2.   Press <enter query>;
3.   Move the cursor to the Order Date field;
4.   Type &Date;
5.   Press <execute query>.

The last action will cause Oracle to display the prompt message Query Where?. This means that it has encountered a parameter – &Date – that needs further defining. The operator can now type in:

&Date between '01-FEB-86' and '28-FEB-86'

(see Figure 5.23) and press the carriage return. Oracle now finds all the rows in the Orders table with an OrderDate between these two values.

'Wildcard' characters can also be entered into queries. If %1986 had been entered into the Order Date field, the system would have found all Orders whose value ends with the number 1986 – all the 1986 orders. The % sign indicates a wildcard value. 1%, for instance, will find all the orders placed on the first of the month – all orders whose date begins with 1. Similarly, %FEB% will find all the orders placed in February. It might not have quite the same effect as the query above, as it would find all February orders regardless of the year in which they were placed. Wildcards can only be used with character-type fields. Range values can be used with any type of field.

5.2.2 Updating a table using a form

SQL*Forms allows the data held in the tables over which the forms are built to be altered, subject to the constraints built in by SQL*Plus. For example, it is not permissible in SQL*Plus to update data via a view if the view takes its data from more than one table. Consequently, when a form is built over such a view, any attempt by the operator to update the information displayed will produce an Oracle error. Oracle errors can also be raised when attempting to enter duplicate values into a field over which a unique index has been created. Raising Oracle errors can be rather disconcerting for the form operator, and, as indicated above, it is the responsibility of the designer to use the Specify Validation, Specify Attributes and Trigger Step windows when defining a field to try to shield the operator from these errors.

Providing Oracle will allow it, changing the values in a displayed record is quite straightforward. After the record to be altered has been retrieved by the appropriate query, the operator moves the cursor to the field or fields to be altered, types over them with new values, and presses <commit>. As long as the data entered is valid, Oracle will provide a confirmation that the new record has been committed to the database. To remove a record from the database, the operator first retrieves it by the appropriate query. The cursor is then moved to the first field of the record and <delete record> is pressed, followed by <commit>. Once again, Oracle will give confirmation of the transaction, as long as it is valid.

To enter a new record into the database, the operator needs to move the cursor to a blank line in the relevant block. This may be done by pressing <clear block>. This blanks out the entire block. Sometimes, the operator may wish to have some other data on the form whilst entering new data. In this case <next record> can be pressed until the cursor reaches a blank line. Alternatively, the <insert record> key can be used. Values can now be typed onto the screen for each field in the new record. Once the record is complete, <commit> is pressed and the record will be inserted into the underlying table, if it is valid. Rather than having to press <commit> each time a new record is entered, a set of records can be inserted: after entering the new values onto the screen, the operator presses <next record> and enters another set of values. None of these records are written to the database until the <commit> function is activated.

When the operator leaves a form using the <exit> function, the software will prompt them if there are any transactions in its working space that have not been committed. The operator can choose whether or not to have them written to the database.

5.3   Re-defining function keys

At the moment, our form has two blocks which are queried independently of each other. The last of the design modifications enables the OrderNo in the Details block to be a duplicate of the OrderNo in the Heading block. However, to display the details of items on a particular order, the operator needs to execute a query on the Heading block, then move to the Details block and press <execute query> again.

What should happen is that every time a query is entered in the Heading block, the Details block should execute a query based on the order number entered. This can be made to happen by re-defining the function key <enter query> on the Heading block. To re-define a function key, the designer enters the Screen Painter for a given block and presses the <select block> button. Pressing the <define> button now brings up the Define Block window depicted in Figure 5.24. From

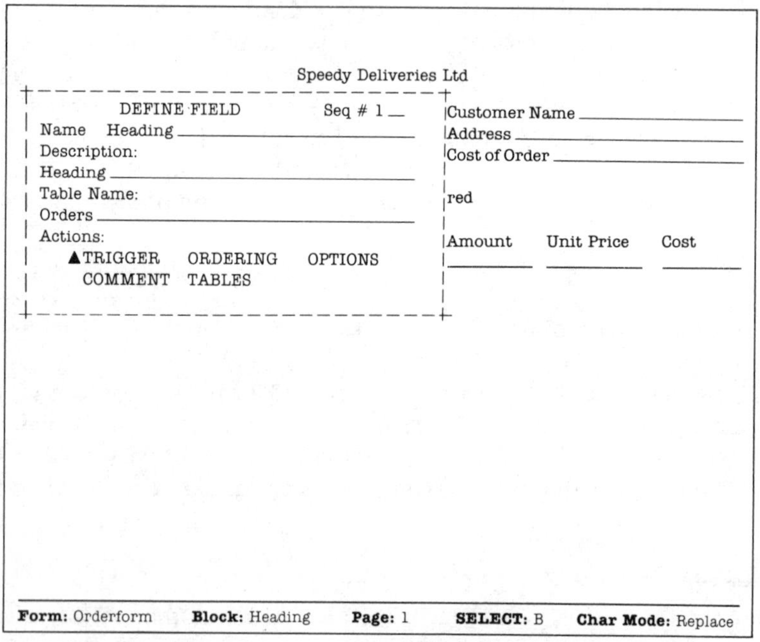

```
                          Speedy Deliveries Ltd
  +-----------------------------------------+
  |      DEFINE FIELD        Seq # 1 __    |Customer Name_____
  | Name   Heading_____     |Address_____
  | Description:                            |Cost of Order_____
  | Heading_____ |
  | Table Name:                             |red
  | Orders_____           |
  | Actions:                                |Amount    Unit Price   Cost
  |   ▲TRIGGER   ORDERING    OPTIONS        |_____  _____  _____
  |    COMMENT   TABLES                     |
  +-----------------------------------------+



  Form: Orderform    Block: Heading    Page: 1    SELECT: B    Char Mode: Replace
```

Figure 5.24   The Define Field window.

here, the Trigger action should be <selected>. This brings up the Choose Trigger window as described above. At the block level, triggers can be defined for when functions are activated. The <enter query> function is known internally by SQL*Forms by the name Entqry and is activated by the button named Key-Entqry. Therefore, to re-define this function, Key-Entqry must be given as the trigger name and the Create action <select>ed. This will bring up the Trigger Step window.

When <enter query> is activated on the Heading block the following functions should be performed:

1.   <next block> to jump to the Details block;

2.   <clear block> to clear the Details block;

3.   <previous block> to jump back to the Heading block;

4.   <entqry> to allow the operator to enter the appropriate search parameters, including the OrderNo;

5.   <next block> to jump back to the Details block. At this point, the validation on OrderNo that was specified in 5.1.3.7 above will cause the heading OrderNo to be copied across to the Details OrderNo;

6.   <execute query> to execute a query of the Details block based on this copied OrderNo value;

7.   <previous block> to return control to the Heading block.

To achieve all of this, the following text has to be entered into the Trigger Step for Key-Entqry:

&EXEMACRO NXTBLK;CLRBLK;PRVBLK;ENTQRY;NXTBLK;
    EXEQRY;PRVBLK;

&EXEMACRO indicates to the SQL*Forms software the text that follows will consist of a number of function calls. NXTBLK;CLRBLK; PRVBLK;ENTQRY;NXTBLK;EXEQRY;PRVBLK are the internal codes for the functions described above. The semi-colon that appears between each function call is a required piece of syntax. The effects of this are shown in Figure 5.25.

From now on, every time a query is executed on the Heading block, records will be automatically retrieved in the Details block that are related to it. The full list of function codes can be found in the SQL*Forms manual. For the two blocks to be fully co-ordinated, triggers will also have to be written that re-define the <execute query>, <next record> and <previous record> keys in the Heading block.

There is also a problem with the trigger written on the field Amount in the Details block. This trigger requires the database tables

```
                        Speedy Deliveries Ltd

    Order No 1  _____     Customer Name  P. Jones _____
    Customer 1  _____     Address        Leeds _____
    Date        24-JAN-86              Cost of Order   88.85_____



    Order No    Stockno     Description    Amount      Unit Price    Cost
    1 _____  1 _____  Bolts _____   55 _____   _____ .15   ____ 8.25
    1 _____  3 _____  Nails _____   124 _____  _____ .65   ____ 80.60
    _____    _____    _____       _____    _____      _____
    _____    _____    _____       _____    _____      _____
    _____    _____    _____       _____    _____      _____
    _____    _____    _____       _____    _____      _____
    _____    _____    _____       _____    _____      _____
    _____    _____    _____       _____    _____      _____
    _____    _____    _____       _____    _____      _____



    Char Mode: Replace                Page: 1                 Count: '2
```

Figure 5.25   Execution of a query on OrderNo 1 using the fully
modified version of OrderForm.

Orderlines and Stock to be examined in order that the total cost of the
order currently displayed in the Heading block may be calculated every
time an amount is entered into the Details block (Section 5.1.3.6 above).
However, when an amount is entered onto the form, its record is not
committed to the database until the <commit> key is depressed. Thus,
the total calculated will be for all the OrderLines *except* for the one
currently being entered! Thus, instead of a post-change trigger on the
Amount field, what is required is a block-level trigger on the <commit>
key for the Details block. This trigger will comprise three steps:

1.   The macro command Commit to write the record to the database;
2.   The select Trigger (as described in Section 5.1.3.6) to calculate and
     enter the cost of the order in the Heading block;
3.   The macro command Commit to write this new total cost to the
     database.

In this chapter, we have only looked at a subset of the facilities available
in SQL*Forms. However, these are probably the most commonly used
of these facilities, and they will have given the reader a realistic flavour
of the system. A more complete description of the various windows
is supplied in the SQL*Forms Windows Summary appendix.

Key points

- A form in SQL*Forms consists of *blocks, fields* and *triggers.*
- A block is built over an underlying database table and its fields are initially derived from the columns in that table.
- Triggers may be written that allow fields to be inserted into a block that are not derived directly from its underlying table using a specially extended form of the SQL syntax.
- Information may be cross-referenced between blocks by use of triggers and validation specification parameters.
- Key functions in SQL*Forms may be modified by the use of triggers that use key function codes.
- A form may be used for the querying, updating, deleting and inserting of data in an Oracle database, subject to the constraints that a form designer has built into a form.

EXERCISE

Design a form consisting of two blocks: Stock and Orders, built over the Stock and OrderLines tables respectively. On the form will be the following fields:

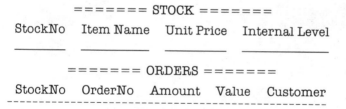

```
======= STOCK =======
StockNo   Item Name   Unit Price   Internal Level
_____   _____   _____    _____

======= ORDERS =======
StockNo   OrderNo   Amount   Value   Customer
-----------------------------------------------------
```

Stock is a single line block whereas Orders should be a ten-line block. The Customer field in Orders is derived from a trigger that relates the OrderNo on the form to a Customer Name in Customers via the CustomerNo that is connected to the same OrderNo in the Orders table. The Value field is derived from multiplying the Amount on an OrderLine by its corresponding price in the Stock table. The two blocks should be tied together via the Stockno and block-level triggers should be written which ensure that when a query is entered onto the Stock block, all Orders relating to that item are retrieved into the Orders block.

Six
Further Aspects of SQL

In the previous chapter on SQL, the way in which the Select operator subsumes the eight basic operators of relational algebra was examined. The functioning of the Insert, Update and Delete operators was also described. In this chapter, some further variations of these operators will be looked at. Most of these are available in 'standard' SQL (the version of SQL that is common to both Oracle and DB2). Those that are restricted to Oracle software will be indicated as such. The examples of output will be based on the tables built in the previous chapter on SQL.

6.1 Built-in functions

The SQL Select command can be used for processing as well as retrieving data. This is achieved by the use of built-in functions. For instance, the Count function is provided to return a tally of the number of rows in a table that satisfy a given condition. To find the number of rows in the Customers table, the command:

    Select Count (*) from Customers;

will return the output:

    COUNT(*)

        5

This was a count without any constraining conditions, so the result represents a count of *all* the rows in Customers. If the command

    Select Count(*)
    from Customers
    where Address = 'Leeds';

was given instead, the result would be:

    COUNT(*)

        2

as the count has been limited to include only those rows which have an Address value of Leeds.

The Count function can also be used with the Distinct clause. The command:

    Select Count (Distinct Stockno)
    from OrderLines;

will return:

    COUNT (DISTINCT STOCKNO)

                    5

indicating the number of different Stockno values that exist in the OrderLines table.

Other functions provided in standard SQL are Sum, Avg, Max and Min. For instance,

    Select Sum (Amount)
    from OrderLines
    where Stockno = 3;

will return:

    SUM(AMOUNT)

        370

This represents the total of all amounts in the OrderLines table placed for orders placed against item 3. To find the average level of orders against item 3, the command

```
Select Avg (Amount)
from OrderLines
where Stockno = 3;
```

will give:

```
AVG(AMOUNT)
----------------
   123.3333333
```

MAX and MIN return respectively the maximum values and minimum values for a given attribute. For instance, the command

```
Select Max(Amount), Min(Amount)
from OrderLines
where Stockno = 3;
```

will give:

```
MAX(AMOUNT)    MIN(AMOUNT)
----------------  ----------------
        234            12
```

representing the highest and lowest order levels placed against item 3.

The Oracle software additionally provides the Stddev and Variance functions to return the standard deviation and variances of a given set of values under a column. These functions are not commonly found in other SQL-based products.

It is worth noting here how the output displays the name of the Selected function at the top of the relevant column. The SQL*Plus Col command can be used to force a more acceptable output. For instance, the SQL*Plus command:

```
Col Sum(Amount) Heading 'Sum of All Order Amounts'
```

will now cause the SQL command:

```
Select Sum(Amount)
from OrderLines;
```

to give the following output:

```
Sum of All Order Amounts
----------------------------
                    1014
```

The above queries return a single result. It is possible to return a set of results from a function. If instead of the total order amount for just one item, it was required for the total order amounts for *each* item to be displayed, the SQL Group By operator would be used. The following command:

```
Select Stockno, Sum (Amount)
from OrderLines
Group By Stockno;
```

will give:

STOCKNO	SUM(AMOUNT)
1	124
2	47
3	370
4	170
5	303

The Group By operator logically re-arranges the table specified in the From part of the query into groups determined by the column(s) specified in Group By. Thus, in the above query, the OrderLines table is partitioned into groups of rows with the same Stockno values. The function specified in the Select line is now executed on each of these groups.

Constraints can be put on which groups of rows are processed using the Having clause. For instance, if this information was only required for items against which there have been more than two orders placed, we can say:

```
Select Stockno, Sum(Amount)
from OrderLines
Group By Stockno
Having Count(*) > 2;
```

giving:

STOCKNO	SUM(AMOUNT)
1	124
3	370
4	170
5	303

as these are the only groups of rows which contain more than two rows. Having is to groups what Where is to individual rows, in that it eliminates groups from a query whereas Where eliminates rows. Having may only be used where a Group By command has been given.

6.2 Tuple variables

In an SQL query such as

    Select Custname
    from Customers;

the from part specifies the table from which the data is to be extracted. What we are, in fact, specifying here is a *tuple variable*. A tuple variable is one that is said to *range over* a given table, that is, a variable whose only permitted values are rows of that table. In SQL, the name of the table over which the variable ranges is, by default, the same as the name of the specified table. However, it is possible to change this default. Some queries require rows to be drawn from a table as a result of comparing one set of rows within a table with another set of rows drawn from the same table. In order to specify such queries, the use of tuple variables is advisable.

For instance, to find those customers who had the same address involves taking the Customers table and comparing it with *itself* to find all those rows with the same address. This can be achieved by the following query:

    Select First.Custname, Second.Custname, First.Address
    from Customers First, Customers Second
    where First.Address = Second.Address;

giving:

CUSTNAME	CUSTNAME	ADDRESS
P. Jones	P. Jones	Leeds
B. Smith	B. Smith	Leeds
P. Jones	B. Smith	Leeds
B. Smith	P. Jones	Leeds
K. Green	K. Green	Colombo
A. Chan	A. Chan	Hong Kong

In the query above, two tuple variables with the names First and Second, each of which range over the Customers table. This was specified by the from clause, where the table name was given followed by a variable name. The Where clause then constrained the output to include only those rows in each of the variables that have the same address as a row in the other variable.

At the moment, the output result has a certain amount of redundancy. For instance, it says that each Customer has the same address as himself/herself! Also, when a match is found it is displayed twice because it will have been found once when one variable is scanned and then once when the other variable is scanned. We can eliminate this quite simply by constraining the output to just those rows where the Custno in First is less than the Custno in Second, thus:

```
Select First.Custname, Second.Custname, First.Address
from Customers First, Customers Second
where First.Address = Second.Address
and First.Custno < Second.Custno;
```

giving:

CUSTNAME	CUSTNAME	ADDRESS
P. Jones	B. Smith	Leeds

6.3   Nested queries

SQL provides the facility to write queries within queries. For instance, to find the CustNos of all of all those customers who have ordered item 3, we could give the command:

```
Select Distinct CustNo
from Orders
where OrderNo in
      (Select OrderNo
      from OrderLines
      where StockNo = 3);
```

giving:

CUSTNO
1
2

The second Select statement above is known as a *subquery*. A subquery is one that is nested inside another by the use of brackets. The syntax rules for subqueries are the same as for standard queries, and the result is the same – the set of rows that satisfies the given query is displayed. Because a subquery yields a set of rows, a predicate such as In can be used to constrain the set of rows that satisfy the outer query. Thus, in the above statement, only those Custnos from Orders are returned which belong to rows whose Ordernos happen to be members of the set of Ordernos returned by the subquery, that is, who have placed an order against item 3.

The In predicate can be negated by placing Not before it. For example, to find the Custnos of those Customers who have not ordered item 3, the following command could be used

```
Select Distinct CustNo
from Orders
where OrderNo not in
        (Select OrderNo
        from OrderLines
        where StockNo = 3);
```

Statements can be nested to multiple levels. If we wished to find the names to go with the customer numbers listed by the above command, the following instruction could be given:

```
Select Custname
from Customers
where Custno in
        (Select Custno from Orders
        where Orderno in
                (Select Orderno
                from OrderLines
                where Stockno = 3));
```

The resulting output would be:

CUSTNAME

P. Jones
A. Chan

These queries could also be written as JOINS. For example, the commands

```
Select Distinct CustNo
from Orders, OrderLines
where Orders.OrderNo = OrderLines.OrderNo
and StockNo = 3;
```

and

```
Select CustName
from Customers, Orders, OrderLines
where Customers.CustNo = Orders.CustNo
and Orders.OrderNo = OrderLines.OrderNo
and StockNo = 3;
```

give exactly the same results as the queries above. Any Join query can be re-written as a nested query (but not all nested queries can be written as Joins). Both are equally correct, and it is partly a matter of personal taste as to which is more suitable.

Comparison operators other than In can be used with nested queries. The simple comparison operators such as =,<,and>, can be used when it is known that the subquery will yield exactly one value. For instance, to find all the customers with the same address as P. Jones, we could say:

```
Select Custname
from Customers
where Address =
        (Select Address
        from Customers
        where CustName = 'P. Jones');
```

giving:

```
CUSTNAME
------------
P. Jones
B. Smith
```

(Of course, this command would raise an error if there were more than one Customer with the name P. Jones because the subquery would yield more than one row.)

To find those item orders whose values are greater than average, the following command could be used:

```
Select * from OrderLines
where Amount >
        (Select Avg(Amount)
        from OrderLines);
```

giving:

ORDERNO	STOCKNO	AMOUNT
1	3	124
2	4	125
3	3	234
3	5	145
4	5	125

In this example, a function was used in the subquery which will only ever yield one result. Therefore, the simple comparison operators can be used against its result with confidence.

Subqueries can also be used with the other SQL operators. For instance, if a new table LeedsCustomers was created which consisted of the names and numbers of only those customers with a Leeds address a whole set of records could be created for this table with a single Insert command thus:

```
Insert into LeedsCustomers
Select Custno, Custname
from Customers
where Address = 'Leeds';
```

A table can be updated by means of a subquery. For instance,

```
Update OrderLines
Set Amount = 0
Where Orderno in
        (Select Orderno
        from Customers, Orders
        where Orders.Custno = Customers.Custno
        and Address = 'Leeds');
```

would set all order levels for LeedsCustomers to zero.

The Delete operator also allows the use of subqueries. To remove all those customers who have not placed an order, the following command would be used:

```
Delete from Customers
where Custno not in
        (Select Custno from Orders);
```

6.4   Wildcard characters

It is not always possible when formulating a query to be precisely sure of the search criteria for that query. In particular, when using character fields, one may wish to retrieve rows that only satisfy a partial match of a given value. SQL provides the Like operator for these sorts of queries.

Suppose, for instance, it was necessary to find all those customers whose address starts with the letter 'L'. This could be achieved with the following query:

```
Select Custname, Address
from Customers
where Address Like 'L%';
```

which would give

```
CUSTNAME   ADDRESS
----------------------
P. Jones   Leeds
B. Smith   Leeds
```

In this example, the % sign acts as a wildcard, telling the system to find all those rows where the Address value starts with the letter 'L', followed by any number of characters.

The % sign can be used to indicate an 'ending with' condition, as in

```
Select Custname
from Customers
with Custname like '%an';
```

which gives:

```
CUSTNAME
------------
Chan
Khan
```

Here, the % sign indicates those rows whose Custname value ends with the letters 'an', preceded by any number of characters. % can also be used to find occurrences of character strings within words. For instance, the query

```
Select Custname
from Customers
where Custname like 'S%';
```

will yield no records. This is because we have included initials as part of the Custname value for each customer. As there are no customers whose initial is S, no rows are returned. To find those customers who have the letter S anywhere in their name, we would say:

```
Select Custname
from Customers
where Custname like '%S%';
```

which would give:

```
CUSTNAME
------------
B. Smith
```

The number of characters that is required to precede or follow the % sign in order to satisfy a given query can be specified to be any number, including zero. Blanks can be used as wildcard characters instead. These have the effect of forcing a specific number of characters to be present within a string in order that it may satisfy a query. The query:

    Select Custname, Address
    from Customers
    where Address like 'L----';

will give:

    CUSTNAME   ADDRESS
    ------------ ----------
    P. Jones   Leeds
    B. Smith   Leeds

The use of blanks in this query forces the Oracle to only return those rows whose address value starts with L and contains *four* other characters, each blank representing a character. Thus the query

    Select Custname, Address
    from Customers
    where Address like 'L-----'

will not retrieve any rows, because there are no rows with an address value that starts with L and is then succeeded by five characters.

Blanks can be placed in front of and around characters in the same way as the % sign. The two wildcard characters can be used together. For instance, to find all those stock items whose names start with any sequence of characters, but which must have the letter e followed by two other letters at the end, we would say:

    Select Sname
    from Stock
    where Sname like '%e--';

This will give

    SNAME

    Spanners
    Screws

6.5   The use of Null

In SQL, a row may be created without any values assigned to one or more of its columns. Those columns, which have no value assigned to them, are not left simply as blanks or zeroes. Instead, they are assigned the value Null. Null cannot be 'equal to' anything else, even itself. The presence of a Null value in a row can be detected by the Is operator so,

    Select * from Customers
    where Address is Null;

gives:

    CUSTNO   CUSTNAME   ADDRESS
    ----
        5   A. Khan

If in the last line of this command, we said:

    where Address = Null;

no records would be retrieved. Since Null cannot be equal to anything, it follows that trying to find something that is equal to Null will always fail. Null can be used as a comparison value with any of the SQL operators. For instance, this customer can be given an address as follows:

    Update Customers
    Set Address = 'Manchester'
    where Address is null;

    The previous Select command will now yield no records, as there are now no records in Customers with a Null value for Address. Conversely, the command:

    Select * from Customers
    where Address is not null;

will now display the entire table.
    Null can be explicitly assigned as a value. For instance, if we wanted to delete the name of an item from our Stock table but at the same time preserving the rest of the row, we could say:

    Update Stock
    Set Sname = Null
    where Sno = 3;

In this command, an attribute value is being specifically set to be 'equal to' something – the value NULL. In this case, the = sign *is* required. The phrase

    SName is Null

would be a syntactic mistake, and cause an error message to be delayed.

The widths of columns in a table can only be reduced when they have no values assigned to them. Should it become necessary once a table is active to reduce the size of any of its columns, the value for that column should first be set to Null for every row in the table. Suppose, for instance, that we wished to change the definition for the Sname column in the Stock table from 20 characters wide to 12. To do this a temporary table would need to be set up to hold all the current Sname values and their corresponding Snos:

```
Create Table Temp
(Stockno Integer,
Sname Char(20));
```

Then these values would have to be copied over from the Stock table with an Insert command:

```
Insert into Temp
Select Stockno,Sname
from Stock;
```

These two steps mean that the names of all the current Sname values with their corresponding Snos have been saved. This is very important because all the Sname values must now be removed from Stock thus:

```
Update Stock
Set Sname = Null;
```

The definition of the Sname attribute can now be Modifyed thus:

```
Alter Table Stock
Modify Sname Char(12);
```

All that remains now is to copy back the new Sname values to Stock:

```
Update Stock
Set Sname =
    (Select Sname from Temp
    where Temp.Sno = Stock.Sno);
```

and to destroy the temporary table:

```
Drop Table Temp;
```

6.6   The Exists operator

SQL provides the Exists operator which acts as an *existential quantifier*. It returns a value 'true' if, and only if, the result of a subquery is not an empty set. For instance, the query:

```
Select Distinct Custno
from Orders
where exists
    (Select * from OrderLines
    where Stockno = 3
    and OrderLines.Orderno = Orders.Orderno);
```

is another way of finding all members of Customers who have ordered item 3. It returns those Custnos in the Orders table for which it *is* true that a row exists in the OrderLines table for Stockno 3 with the corresponding Orderno on it. To find the numbers of those who have *not* ordered Stockno 3, we could say:

```
Select Distinct Custno
from Orders
where not exists
    (Select * from OrderLines
    where Stockno = 3
    and OrderLines.Orderno = Orders.Orderno);
```

A general form for implementing the DIVIDE operation (see Sections 1.2 and 3.2 above) can now be introduced. To find those order numbers in the OrderLines table that are matched against every StockNo in the Stock table, we can say:

```
Select Distinct y.Orderno
from OrderLines y
where not exists
    (Select Stockno from Stock
    minus
    Select Stockno
    from OrderLines z
    where z.orderno = y.orderno);
```

This will yield:

```
ORDERNO
----------
2
3
```

which are the numbers of those orders that are placed against all five items of Stock.

This command involves the use of two *tuple variables*: y and z, both ranging over the OrderLines table. The Select in line one asks for all the distinct Ordernos in table y (the OrderLines table). The **where not exists** constrains this selection to those OrderNos which do not satisfy the nested command. The nested command selects all the StockNos in the Stock table minus all the StockNos in table z which is another image of OrderLines such that the OrderNo in z matches the OrderNo in y. Thus, the nested command yields for each OrderNo in y all those StockNos which it is not matched against. If there are no StockNos against which it is not matched then the where not exists flag is raised and the OrderNo is output. In other words, the query is asking for all those OrderNos for which there are no StockNo items that they have not been matched against.

6.7 The Outer Join

It is sometimes useful to display rows from a Join query which do not actually satisfy the Join condition. For instance, we might wish to display a list of Customers with their order details, and include in that list those Customers who have not actually placed any orders. This form of Join is called the Outer Join and can be coded in Oracle's version of SQL thus:

```
Select Custname, Orderno
from Customers, Orders
where Customers.Custno = Orders.Custno (+);
```

giving:

CUSTNAME	ORDERNO
P. Jones	1
P. Jones	2
K. Green	
A. Chan	3
B. Smith	4
A. Khan	

The + sign instructs the system to set up an imaginary row in the Orders table which contains only null values. Thus, all those Customers in the Customers table who cannot be joined to a row in the Orders table are instead joined to this imaginary row and displayed.

The Outer Join feature is exclusive to Oracle, and is not currently available in any other mainstream SQL-based system, including DB2.

6.8 Concluding note

It may have been noticed by the reader that the word 'could' rather than 'would' has been used as a preface to many of the examples in this chapter. This is because many of these queries can be coded in more than one way.

This renders the creation of optimization algorithms very difficult for an SQL-based system. The optimizer has to attempt to set up the same optimal access paths to find a set of data that can be specified in many different ways. As a result of this, the user will find that, with large files, the coding of a query will have an effect on its speed of execution, which is not an ideal situation. In particular, the use of not exists is usually preferable to not in. This is because the latter works on the principle of returning those values that do not match against the entire set of values returned by a subquery whereas the former works by *eliminating* values from a result set on the basis of a Boolean flag raised on a given condition in a subquery evaluating to 'true'. This sort of consideration is undesirable as it distracts the user from the problem to be solved and forces them to pay attention to the detail of the coding instead, which runs contrary to one of the fundamental *raisons d'etre* for a 'fourth generation' system, like Oracle. The ability to code the same query in many different ways is a drawback of SQL. This and other drawbacks of SQL are discussed in greater detail by Date (1987). Notwithstanding these shortcomings, SQL is a versatile and powerful database language which is now well established as the *de facto* industry standard for relational systems.

Key points

- SQL provides a number of standard functions for performing arithmetic operations on the data in a table.

- Tables in SQL may be re-named in an SQL query by the use of tuple variables, thus allowing a table to processed against itself.

- SQL allows the use of nested queries to yield sets of values at different levels within an SQL Select command.

- 'Fuzzy' searches can be performed in SQL using wildcard characters.

- The truth value of a nested query can be tested by use of the Exists operator.

- Oracle provides the outer join extension to SQL to enable those rows to be yielded from a query that do not meet the join condition.

EXERCISES

6.1 Using the standard SQL functions, write SQL statements which will:
1. Display how many orders have been placed against the item screws;
2. Calculate the average value of all orders placed against bolts;
3. Display the highest, lowest and average amount for orders placed against spanners.

6.2 Re-write the command file for your answer to exercise 4.2, so that instead of a line for every OrderLine placed, the output consists of a line for each city summarizing the total value of all orders placed per city thus:

City   Value of All Orders
----   -------------------

6.3 Write an SQL statement that generates three columns from the OrderLines table indicating those pairs of OrderNos that are placed against the same Stockno.

6.4 Write
1. A nested query;
2. A query that explicitly uses Join operations to display the names of all customers who have ordered spanners.

6.5 Write an SQL statement that displays the names of all customers
1. with the letter 'o' in their address;
2. whose name starts with the letter 'K';
3. whose address starts with the letter 'H' and ends with the letter 'g'.

6.6 Write an SQL statement that will display the names of those items that have been ordered by every customer.

6.7 In this chapter, the query *Find all Customers who have not ordered Item 3* was satisfied by using both not in and not exists. Which of these queries is most likely to give the more efficient (quicker) response, and why?

6.8 Describe and explain the use of the Outer Join.

Reference

C.J. Date: 'Where SQL Falls Short', *Datamation*, May 1987.

Seven
Report Generation Using SQL*Report

The SQL*Plus software provides a number of *ad hoc* report generation facilities such as the Compute, Break and Col commands discussed in Chapter 4. However, these are limited in their scope. In particular, there is no provision for embedding text into reports generated in SQL*Plus. In order to provide a more powerful report generation facility, Oracle provides the RPF (Report Text Formatter) and RPT (Report Generation) facilities, which together form the SQL*Report module.

The RPF program is a text formatting program that can be used in a stand-alone mode to produce user-defined documents. It is command driven, in that the appearance of the document depends on RPF commands embedded in the text. The RPT progam interprets RPT statements to extract and process data from an Oracle database. Once extracted, this data may be formatted using RPF commands.

Generation of reports in SQL*Report is a two-pass process using these facilities. This is shown diagrammatically in Figure 7.1. The programmer is required to create a *report control file* consisting of RPT statements, RPF formatting commands and user text. This file is first submitted to the RPT program which examines the RPT statements and converts them into data from the underlying database. This creates an interim file containing data, text and formatting commands. This file can

131

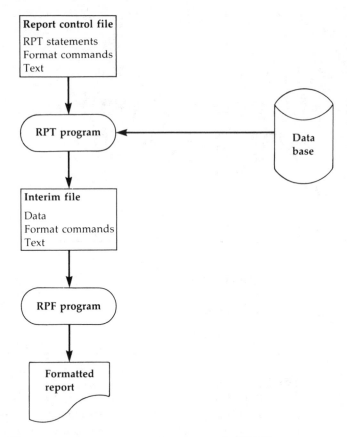

Figure 7.1   The two-pass report generation process in SQL*Report.

now be submitted to the RPF program which interprets the formatting commands to produce a finished document.

In this chapter, the generation of a simple report using the RPT and RPF utilities will be examined. First how text can be formatted using RPF commands embedded in a document will be discussed, followed by a discussion concerning how data can be inserted from an Oracle database into this document using RPT statements. RPF and RPT are facilities that are invoked at operating system level. The preparation of the report control file is also done at this level, using a system-supplied text editor or word processor.

7.1   Preparation of a document using RPF

The exercise that will be undertaken in this chapter will be the preparation of a report from the Customer/Orders/Stock database that indicates the total amount of each stock item ordered along with the

```
+------------------------------------------------+
| Dear John,                                     |
|                                                |
|     Please find below a per item summary of the|
| total amounts and values of all outstanding orders. |
|                                                |
| Best regards,                                  |
| Daphne                                         |
|                                                |
|                                                |
| Itemno    Itemname    Amount     Order         |
|                       Ordered    Values        |
|                                                |
|                                                |
|    ___      _____      ____       ____         |
|    ___      _____      ____       ____         |
|    ___      _____      ____       ____         |
|    ___      _____      ____       ____         |
|    ___      _____      ____       ____         |
|                                                |
|                                                |
| Total value of all orders: _____            |
+------------------------------------------------+
```

Figure 7.2   General format of sales report.

value of these orders. The report will be prefaced by a letter to the sales manager, Mr John Avarice. At the end of the report will be a summary total of all the order values. Thus, the report will have the general format indicated in Figure 7.2.

The text at the start of the report can be specified by preparing the following document:

```
#DT 1 13 65 #
#T 1
#PAGE 6 58
#CUL Sales Summary Report
#S 2
Dear John #P
Please find below a per item summary of the total amounts
and values of all outstanding orders.
#B
Best Regards, Daphne
#TE
```

This document has a number of embedded RPF commands, each indicated here by a preceding # symbol – the '.' symbol may also be used. The effects of these commands are as follows:

1. DT (*Define table*). The output of an RPF document is formatted within a series of user-defined *tables*. A table consists of a series of columns. In the DT command above, the first number – 1 – identifies the table as table 1, and the next two numbers – 13, 65 – indicate the margins of the single column that comprises this table. Thus, all output that uses table 1 as a frame is formatted within a single column that spans the positions 13 to 65. These are counted in from the left-hand side of the page. There is a default RPF table that consists of a single column spanning position 1 to position 255.

    Because a table can consist of an inderminate number of columns, DT is a closed command. That is, it requires the '#' or '.' symbol to start it and to terminate it.

2. T (*Table*). This command invokes the table to be used for the next set of output. T 1 indicates that the table defined in the DT 1 command is to be used for the next set of output. When a table is invoked by the T command, it is automatically placed within the last column of the last table to have been invoked. At this stage, only the default table exists, so table 1 is placed within the margins (1 to 255) of the default table. The next table to be invoked will be placed within the margins (13 to 65) of table 1 – see Figure 7.3.

3. Page. The Page command is used to indicate the top and bottom margins of each page of output. It requires two parameters: the first one indicates the number of blank lines to be inserted at the top of each page, and the second one indicates how many lines may be output before the next page is skipped to. RPF assumes that all pages have a length of 66 lines, thus the Page command above will cause 6 blank lines at the top of each page, followed by 58 lines of output with 2 blank lines at the bottom of each full page.

4. CUL (*Centre underline*). This self-explanatory command indicates that the next line of text is to be centred in the page and underlined.

5. S (*Skip*). This command instructs RPF to skip a specified number of lines before printing the next text. Thus, S 2 means Skip 2 lines.

6. P (*Paragraph*). This command indicates that the next piece of text should be indented five spaces in from the left of the current column.

7. B (*Blank line*). The B command has the same effect as an S 1 command – it will cause a blank line to be output before the next text.

8.   TE (*Table end*). This indicates the end of a table. However, note that when a table is ended, the last column to be invoked is still in force.

Single-column tables are suitable for the output of continuous prose such as a letter. The output of data, on the other hand, usually requires a multi-column table. The body of the report above has four columns. These can be specified as follows:

```
#DT 2        1 6   10 19   24 30   34 43 #
#T 2
#S 3
#R ItemNo      #NC
#R ItemName  #NC
#R Amount    #N
#R Ordered   #NC
#R Order     #N
#R Values    #NC
```

These commands set up a second table consisting of four columns spanning positions 1 to 6, 10 to 19, 24 to 30 and 34 to 43 respectively. Note that these represent *offset* positions only. If this table is invoked after table 1 has been invoked and ended, then the actual positions of these columns will depend on the value of the left-hand position of the last invoked column of table 1. In our current example, this is position 13, so the first column in table 2 will occupy positions 13 to 18 and so on. This is shown in Figure 7.3.

A number of commands follow that set up headings for each column. The #R command indicates that the text following is to be right-justified within the column. #NC means 'Skip to the next column', #N means 'Skip to the next line within the current column'. Thus, the first #R command indicates the right-justified heading ItemNo for the first column of the report. This is immediately followed by the #NC command indicating the end of text for this heading. The next heading, ItemName, is set up in the same way. Amount Ordered is a two-line

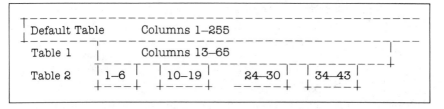

Figure 7.3 RPF table definitions used in sales report column Definitions for each table are taken as offsets from the left-hand margin of the most recently invoked table.

Sales Summary Report

Dear John,

    Please find below a per item summary of the total amounts and values of all outstanding orders.

Best regards, Daphne

ItemNo	ItemName	Amount Ordered	Order Values

Figure 7.4   Report without data.

heading, so the #N command must be inserted after the word Amount, indicating that the next piece of text, Ordered, is to be placed on the next line in the same column. The final column is set up in the same way. The final #NC command is necessary here to send the text back to the first column, otherwise the next set of text will be printed under the final column.

    The RPF commands above can be entered into a single file and submitted to the RPF program to give the output shown in Figure 7.4. At the moment, of course, there is no data in the report! This will have to be extracted by a series of RPT statements and submitted to some further RPF formatting commands.

7.2   Processing data using RPT

An RPT program has three main elements: data declarations, select macros, and procedural macros.

    The *data declarations* are used to set up the names and formats of the data items that are going to be used in the report. The syntax for their formatting is somewhat similar to the Col command syntax for formatting column-headings in SQL*Plus.

    The *select macros* consist of SQL Select statements that extract data from the database and place it into the data items set up by the data declarations.

    The *procedural macros* consist of a series of commands that control the sequence of output from a report. They may contain calls to other macros, they may cross-refer to the variables set up in the data declarations and they may have embedded RPF formatting commands. A report may have up to three procedural macros: a *head*, a *body* and a *foot*. The head is executed for the first line of output, the body for the second line through to the last lines of output and the foot is (optionally) executed after the body.

    For the report above, data declarations are required for variables to hold the numbers, names, amounts and values of each stock item. A variable is also needed to hold the total of all these values. These can be set up with the following RPT statements:

```
.Database AccountName
.Declare itemno 099999
.Declare itemname a10
.Declare amounts 999999
.Declare values $B99,999.99
.Declare totvalues $B999,999.99
```

RPT, like RPF, uses the '.' or '#' symbol to indicate the start of an RPT command. In this text, we will use the '.' symbol to pre-fix RPT commands and the '#' symbol for RPF commands to distinguish between the two.

First of all, the Database statement is used to name the Oracle account from which the data will be extracted, (a dummy accountname value has been inserted here.) A number of data declarations follow which name and format the variables that are to be used in the report. itemno and amounts are indicated using as a numeric variable the number 9, with the number of digits specifying the maximum allowable column width. The first digit on itemno is 0, indicating that leading zeroes are to be inserted for those numbers less than the specified width. itemname is specified by using as an alphanumeric variable the 'a' character, the number 10 indicating its maximum allowable width. values and totvalues are numeric items which will be output with a leading '$' sign. The ',' indicates that a comma is to be placed at the specified positions. The 'B' indicates that if the value of the variable is zero, then the space is to be left blank rather than a zero output.

The report requires two select macros: one to select the numbers, names amounts and values of all orders on a per item basis and put them into the appropriate variables, second to calculate the total value of all orders. These can be encoded as follows:

```
.Define  selitems
     Select   OrderLines.StockNo,SName,Sum(Amount),
              Sum(Amount*SPrice)
     Into     ItemNo, ItemName, Amounts, Values
     From     OrderLines, Stock
     Where    OrderLines.StockNo = Stock.StockNo
     Group By OrderLines.StockNo, SName
     ..
.Define Totals
     Select  Sum(Amount*SPrice)
     Into    TotValues
     From    OrderLines, Stock
     Where   OrderLines.StockNo = Stock.StockNo
     ..
```

These two macros both use a SQL Select statement to extract the relevant data from the database and place it into an ordered set of RPT variables indicated by the Into line. The '..' indicates the end of the macro.

There now remain the head, body and foot procedural macros. The head section macro sets up the column headings and calls the body macro for the first line of output. The body macro displays each of the variables under the appropriate column. The foot calls the 'totals' macro and displays its result. Thus the main part of the report looks like this:

```
.Define head
    #DT 2         1  6   10 19   24 30   34 43  #
    #T 2
    #S 3
    #R ItemNo      #NC
    #R ItemName    #NC
    #R Amount      #N
    #R Ordered     #NC
    #R Order       #N
    #R Values      #NC
    #B
.body
..

.Define body
    .Print ItemNo #NC
    .Print ItemName #NC
    .Print Amounts #NC
    .Print Values #NC
..

.Define Foot
    #TE
    #S 4
    Total Value of all Orders :
    .Execute Totals
    .Print TotValues
..

.Report SelItems Body Head Foot
#TE
.Stop
```

The head macro simply sets out the column headings using the same RPF commands as before. The call to Body is necessary here as the Body macro only executes for the second through to the last line of output.

Thus the first line of data yielded by the SelItems macro would otherwise be lost. Alternatively, explicit Print statements could have been put into the Head macro, but this would have represented a wasteful duplication of effort in this case!

The Body macro uses Print to display the variable values under each column in turn, moving from one column to the next using the RPF NC command.

The Foot macro disables the column settings with the RPF TE command and calls up the Totals macro to yield a summary total for display, along with an appropriate message.

Once all the macros are defined, the Report command can be used to activate the RPT statements. First of all, the SelItems macro is activated to yield a set of values to be assigned to the given variables. Then the body, head and foot macros are activated to output these variables in an appropriate sequence. The Stop command indicates the end of the report.

7.3   Generating the report

The completed Report Control File will look like this:

```
Rem  *************************************
.Rem Report to Sales Manager
.Rem Analysing per item sales to date
.Rem *************************************
.Rem define tables
.Rem *************************************
#DT 1   13 65 #
#DT 2   1 6   10 19   24 30   34 43 #
.Rem *************************************
.Rem Write letter to J. Avarice
.Rem *************************************
#T 1
#Page 6 58
#CUL Sales Summary Report
#S 2
Dear John #P
Please find below a per item summary of the total amounts
and values of all outstanding orders.
#B
Best Regards, Daphne
#S 2
```

```
.Rem Declare Variables
.Database AccountName
.Declare ItemNo 099999
.Declare ItemName a10
.Declare Amounts 999999
.Declare Values $B99,999.99
.Declare TotValues $B999,999.99
.Rem
.Rem
.Rem Define Select Macros
.Define  SelItems
      Select   OrderLines.StockNo,SName,Sum(Amount),
               Sum(Amount*SPrice)
      Into     ItemNo, ItemName, Amounts, Values
      From     OrderLines, Stock
      Where    OrderLines.StockNo = Stock.StockNo
      Group By OrderLines.StockNo, SName
  ..
.Rem
.Define Totals
      Select   sum(amount*SPrice)
      Into     TotValues
      From     OrderLines, Stock
      Where    OrderLines.StockNo = Stock.StockNo
  ..
.Rem
.Rem
.Rem Define Procedural Macros
.Define Head
      #T 2
      #S 3
      #R ItemNo     #NC
      #R ItemName   #NC
      #R Amount     #N
      #R Ordered    #NC
      #R Order      #N
      #R Values     #NC
      #B
.body
  ..
.Define Body
      .Print ItemNo     #NC
      .Print ItemName   #NC
      .Print Amounts    #NC
      .Print Values     #NC
```

```
..
.Define Foot
    #TE
    #S 4
    Total Value of all Orders :
    .Execute Totals
    .Print TotValues

..
.Report SellItems Body Head Foot
#TE
.STOP
```

The RPT REM statement is used here to provide in-line documentation for the program listing. All lines prefixed by the REM statement are effectively ignored by the RPT interpreter and deleted from the interim file submitted to RPF. For the sake of neatness, the DT command for the second table has been taken out of the Head section and placed next to the DT command for the first table.

This control file can now be submitted to the RPT interpreter with a command in the following form:

RPT Inputfilename Outputfilename Oracleaccount/Password

The Inputfilename element is the name of the report control file and the Outputfilename is the name of the interim file to be submitted to RPF. The user must also submit the name of their Oracle account and its password so that the RPT program knows from where to reference the data in the Select macros. If the user has written macros selecting data from tables to which their account does not have access rights, then the RPT program will fail.

If successful, though, the RPT program will produce an interim file consisting of processed data and RPF commands. This file can now be submitted to the RPF program as a command in the format:

RPF Inputfilename Outputfilename Switches

In this case, the Inputfilename will be the name of the interim file generated by RPT. The Outputfilename is the filename to which the completed report is written. There are a number of optional switches that may be invoked to, for instance, direct the output to a line printer or force the output into all upper case. These are listed in Figure 7.5.

The data in our sample Customer/Orders/Stock database will generate the output shown in Figure 7.6 from the report specified in this chapter.

a – All bold face	m – Show dynamic memory usage
b – Bold face underlines	p:n:m – Reverse #'s n to m
d:d – Device is diablo	r – Reverse underlining order
d:v – Device is VT100	s – Spool to line printer
f – Form Feed for page eject	u – Upper case output
i – Initial page eject	w – Enable Wait if device = d or v

Figure 7.5   Table of optional RPF switches.

There are a number of other RPF and RPT statements available to the programmer not covered here. In particular, RPT supplies arithmetic commands to enable further amendments to the values of variables, and If and Goto commands that can alter the sequence of events in a report. There are also Add, Sub, Mul and Div commands to enable arithmetic processing of data without resort to the standard SQL functions. An Ask command is provided which allows parameters to be entered during the execution of a report. SQL*Report can only be used for generating information from a database, it cannot be used to update or alter that database.

Sales Summary Report

Dear John,

Please find below a per item summary of the total amounts and values of all outstanding orders.

Best Regards, Daphne

ItemNo	ItemName	Amount Ordered	Order Values
000001	Bolts	124	$18.60
000002	Nuts	47	$35.25
000003	Nails	370	$240.50
000004	Spanners	170	$809.20
000005	Screws	303	$33.33

Total Value of all Orders: $1,136.88

Figure 7.6   The report with data.

Key points

- Report generation in SQL*Report is a two-phase process using the RPT and RPF programs to process a report control file.

- A report control file consists of RPT statements that extract and process data from an Oracle database and RPF statements that format this data for output.

- A report control file may also contain user text that is subject to RPF formatting commands.

- The output of a report may be customized at run time by a number of optional user switches.

EXERCISES

7.1 Describe the sequence of events necessary to generate a report from an Oracle database using SQL*Report.

7.2 Explain the concept of a *Table* as used in RPF. How can multi-column tables be specified?

7.3 Define the following RPT terms :
   (a) Data declarations;
   (b) Select macros;
   (c) Procedural macros.

7.4 What is the purpose of the RPT Rem statement?

7.5 Write the necessary SQL*Report command file to generate a report that calculates the total value of all Orders on a per Customer basis. The output should be in the form of a memorandum as shown in Figure 7.7.

```
                    MEMORANDUM

From:   The Data Processing Manager
To:   The Managing Director
Subject:   Value of Sales per Customer

    Please find below a summary of the total value of all Orders placed
by each of our Customers.

          Customer Name    Value of Orders Placed
          ---------------- ----------------------
```

Figure 7.7   Format of memorandum for Exercise 7.5.

Eight
Database Administration with Oracle

A live multi-user DBMS implementation requires a database administrator (DBA) to manage the use and enhance the performance of the system.

The database administrator plays both a managerial and a technical role. The person who takes it on is responsible for controlling the use of the system and for ensuring the security and integrity of the data. They must be appraised of the user requirements and liaise with user community in order to monitor the degree to which the system meets these requirements. They are furthermore responsible for assessing and optimizing the performance of an installed system.

To carry out the technical duties, a system has to provide the database administrator with a number of tools. In this chapter, the way in which an Oracle database administrator can carry out the following tasks will be examined:

- Starting and stopping the database
- Enrolling and dropping users
- Backing up and recovering information from the database

145

- Monitoring and enhancing the database performance
- Re-sizing and adding database files.

Some of these tasks can be carried out from within an Oracle DBA account, others require access to the underlying Oracle programs and data files.

In a multi-user system, these underlying programs and data files should be stored in a specially protected operating system account. Oracle users should only be able to execute those programs that are necessary for running their personal Oracle account, such as SQL*Plus, SQL*Forms etc. They should *not* be able to access the underlying database files apart from indirectly through their Oracle account. Neither should they be able to execute any of the programs described in this chapter apart from the EXP and IMP utilities described below. The details of how to achieve this vary from system to system and are referred to in the Oracle *Installation Guides* for the different machines that Oracle software can run on.

As the installation process varies from machine to machine, it will not be examined in this text. Instead, the starting point will be immediately after installation, when the DBA will want to start a live system for the first time.

8.1   Starting and stopping an Oracle database

The IOR program is used to initialize, start and stop an Oracle database. *Database* here means the entire set of accounts and partitions that make up a database, not just the individual user accounts and tables.

8.1.1   Starting up

To start a database for the first time, the DBA gives the operating system level command:

    IOR Init

This command sets up a single partition database ready for use. Any user data already in the database files is destroyed. The Init command is only used when a database has just been installed, when an upgrade has been performed on the Oracle software, or when the operating system files have been re-configured. In the latter two cases, the DBA will have had to ensure that the user data in the system has been backed up.

To re-start an Oracle database, the relevant command is:

    IOR Warm

Unlike the Init option, the Warm option has no effect on the database partitions or any data that is already in the database. Init is sometimes referred to as a *cold* start, as opposed to a *warm* start. Both the Init and Warm options generate the *system global area* and start the *detached processes*.

8.1.1.1 The system global area (SGA)

The sytem global area is a shared area in main memory which is created every time an Oracle system is activated. It is the centre of all activity when the software is running and contains items such as data buffers, lock lists, column caches, table caches and user caches, a cache being, in simple terms, a copy of data held on disk. All user processes access the database via the data structures held in the SGA. The *detached* or *background* processes service the use of the SGA.

The size of the SGA is determined by a series of parameters held in the Init.Ora file supplied with the Oracle software. This file is read each time the database is started up. Some of these parameters are operating-system dependent and should not be amended. Others, such as the location of the first of the database files, can be changed. These *variable* parameters will be discussed at appropriate times later in the chapter.

8.1.1.2 The detached processes

The detached processes are used to govern the SGA. Three of them (BIW, BWR and CLN) are always automatically invoked each time the Oracle software is started. The other one (ARH) is only invoked if the appropriate parameter in the Init.Ora file is set to a non-null value. The actions of these detached processes is as follows:

1. BIW (*Before Image Writer*). This process copies blocks from the Before Image cache buffer in the system global area to the Before Image file. The Before Image (BI) file contains images of all currently used data before changes are made to it. It is used to ensure that any transactions performed on the data are not made permanent until they are explicitly or implicitly committed by the appropriate user command. Transactions are explicitly committed by use of the SQL*Plus Commit command. Implicit commits are made when the user gives a Create Table, Create View, Create Index or Drop Table command or when they log out. When a transaction is committed, the images of the records used are deleted from the BI file, thus making it permanent. Before a transaction is committed, it may be deleted by the SQL*Plus Rollback command. This causes the Oracle software to write the contents of the BI file back to those tables that belong to the user, thus undoing all updates since the last commit. The BI file is also

used for recovery purposes when the system has crashed or been brought down in an emergency. The location of the BI file is one of the parameters held in the Init.Ora file.

2.   **BWR** (*Buffer writer*). This process takes modified blocks from the system global area buffer when space is needed for further blocks and writes these to the database files and also to the After Image files if After Image Journalling has been enabled. After Image Journalling is enabled when the appropriate parameter (After_Image) in Init.Ora is set to a non-zero value. Its purpose is to enable a database to be restored after a system crash. The After_Image parameter records the location of the After Image file.

3.   **CLN** (*Cleanup*). This process periodically scans the system global area to discover whether there are any processes that have terminated abnormally. If it finds any such processes, it uses the BI file to roll back any outstanding transactions belonging to them and logs them off.

4.   **ARH** (*Asynchronous read ahead*). This is an optional process, activated only by setting the Read-Requests parameter in Init.Ora to 5 or more. It copies blocks from the database file into the system global area on behalf of those queries that require a full table scan. ARH reads the blocks in parallel with the execution of the program that processes the retrieved data, thus reducing the time required to complete the query.

The general relationship between the detached processes, the SGA and the stored database is illustrated in Figure 8.1.

DBAs may set up their own parameter file and call it up with a variant of the IOR command thus:

    IOR Warm PFile=CustomFile

where CustomFile is the name of the DBAs self-created parameter file.

8.1.2   Shutting down

To shut down an Oracle database, the command given is:

    IOR Shut

This command checks that there are no Oracle accounts which are currently active. When all the users have logged off, it terminates the detached processes, closes the database files and releases the SGA. This command must be issued by the DBA prior to activities such as re-sizing the database or backing up the database files.

Sometimes, operating circumstances prevent an orderly shut-

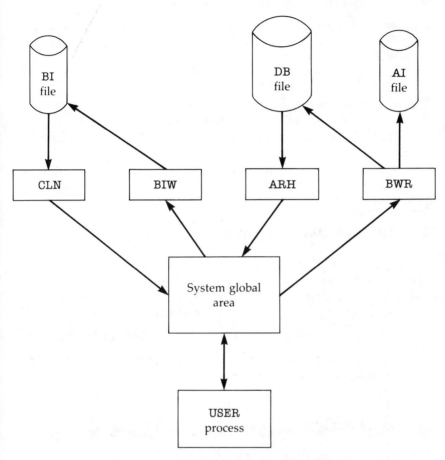

Figure 8.1 The SGA and the detached processes.

down of an Oracle system with the Shut option. In this case, the command:

    IOR Clear

shuts a system down without waiting for the current users to log off. This leaves the user processes 'dangling' in the system, and they must be subsequently terminated at operating system level. It is almost certain that there will be outstanding user transactions that have not been committed to the database. Therefore, the Before Image file will have data in it which will be used by the next warm start to roll back any of these outstanding transactions. For this reason, the Before Image file should never be re-sized after a Clear stop, otherwise the system cannot be re-started. Thus, the Clear option should only be used when absolutely necessary. When a Clear stop has been used and the user processes terminated at the operating system level, it is usually advisable to perform a restricted warm start using the following command:

IOR Warm DBA

This restricts use of the system to those user accounts which have DBA status. This gives the system the chance to 'recover' from the Clear stop. The Shut option should now execute without any difficulty. This restricted warm start is mandatory prior to the DBA performing certain functions such as adding new files to the database or exporting users' data to back-up storage.

8.2   Enrolling and dropping users

User accounts are added to and removed from an Oracle database by means of a variant of the SQL Grant and Revoke commands that is available only to those accounts which have DBA status.

To enrol a user, the format of the Grant command is thus:

Grant {privileges} TO {username} Identified BY {password} ;

The privileges a user may have are Connect, Resource and DBA. Thus, to enroll a user named Jim with the ability to log on to the database and create their own tables using the password 'James', the Grant command would be:

Grant Connect, Resource To Jim Identified By James;

Revoke is used similarly to remove privileges. If, for instance, Jim was to no longer have the ability to create tables, we would say:

Revoke Resource From Jim;

A user is logically removed from the system by Revokeing their Connect privilege. However, their tables still remain physically written to the database files, so that a subsequent re-enrolment will find them restored to the point at which they were removed.

All logged-on users may Grant the Connect privilege to themselves. This allows them to change their passwords, so

Grant Connect To Jim Identified By Jimmy;

executed from Jim's account will change Jim's password from James to Jimmy. However, an attempt by JIM to change anyone else's password would raise an error unless he had been Granted the DBA privilege from a DBA account. A database administrator may wish to change a user's password when it has been mislaid or forgotten. The special user accounts Sys and System are installed with default passwords, and it is the responsibility of the database administrator to log in to these accounts immediately after the database has been initialized and change their passwords in order to protect the data dictionary. These accounts themselves have DBA status and are thus inevitably the first to be used by the database administrator to set up other accounts.

8.3   Backup and recovery

The Database Administrator is responsible for ensuring that the database files are archived at appropriate intervals. This can be done fully from the operating system level, and partially by use of the Oracle EXPort utility.

Oracle accounts with Resource or DBA privileges can use the EXP command to copy to a file which can be archived those database objects that belong to them. EXP can be used in three modes:

(a)   Table
(b)   User
(c)   Full DB.

In Table mode, the user is asked for the names of those tables that they wish to archive. Both the table definitions and the data will be saved. Views, clusters and indexes cannot be saved in this mode.

In User mode, the entire user account, apart from their view definitions, will be saved. When a user with DBA status uses this mode, they can specify accounts other than their own to be archived. Thus, a DBA can use this mode selectively to backup a section of the database.

The Full DB mode is only available to DBA accounts. In this mode, the entire database, apart from those objects belonging to Sys, is archived.

Each of these modes requires the user to specify a name for the archive file. The contents of this file can be re-loaded into a database by any user with Connect and Resource privileges using the IMPort utility. As with EXP, the IMP command can be used to import tables, user accounts or whole databases selectively. These utilities are especially useful when performing tasks such as moving data between one database and another, freeing up space within a database or moving data to an up-graded version of Oracle.

It is worth noting here an implication of the fact that objects belonging to Sys are never EXPorted. This means that the list of Oracle users in Sysuserauth cannot be transferred automatically from one database to another. Thus, an attempt to IMPort a user account may raise an error since that user may not be present in the list of users for the database from where the IMPort has been activated. A database can only be said to be fully backed-up by periodically making a duplicate copy of all the database files at operating system level.

If After Image Journalling has been enabled by the DBA, then the AIJ utility may be used to recover a database which for some reason has suffered a 'fatal' failure. First of all, the DBA must shut down the database and replace the database files with a backup copy of the files made when After Image Journalling was first enabled. The AIJ utility can then be invoked to restore the database as near as possible to its condition just prior to the fatal crash.

AIJ works as a two-pass process. In the first pass, it requests the DBA for each successive journal file and flags all those transactions which were not committed. Unless all the transactions are uncommitted, AIJ then proceeds onto its second pass where it writes all the committed transactions to the database files.

8.4   Monitoring and enhancing database performance

When a database is in use, the Oracle Display System (ODS) may be called up by the database to monitor activity in the system.

The ODS command is given at the operating system level and typically provides the display indicated in Figure 8.2.

From this screen, any of the screens listed can be invoked using the indicated command. The contents of a screen can be saved to a log file by use of the Open <filename> option which may subsequently be closed with the Close command and sent to a hard copy device for detailed perusal at the end of the ODS session. Each screen takes and

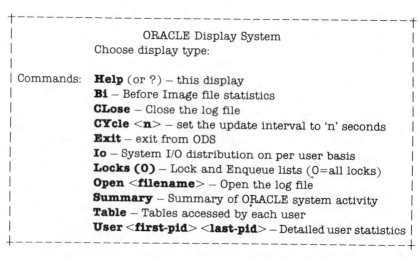

```
+-----------------------------------------------------------------+
|                    ORACLE Display System                        |
|              Choose display type:                               |
|                                                                 |
| Commands:  Help (or ?) – this display                           |
|            Bi – Before Image file statistics                    |
|            CLose – Close the log file                           |
|            CYcle <n> – set the update interval to 'n' seconds   |
|            Exit – exit from ODS                                 |
|            Io – System I/O distribution on per user basis       |
|            Locks (0) – Lock and Enqueue lists (0=all locks)     |
|            Open <filename> – Open the log file                  |
|            Summary – Summary of ORACLE system activity          |
|            Table – Tables accessed by each user                 |
|            User <first-pid> <last-pid> – Detailed user statistics |
+-----------------------------------------------------------------+
```

Figure 8.2   The ODS Display.

displays a series of 'snapshots' of the condition of part of the system. The interval at which these snapshots are taken can be changed with the Cycle command. Allowable intervals range between 1 and 600 seconds.

Brief descriptions of what each screen does are given here. More detailed descriptions are to be found in the Oracle *Database Administrator's Guide*.

1.   The Before Image screen displays information concerning the Before Image file and can be used to determine the amount of space available in the file. This can be used as an 'early warning system' to the database administrator as to the likelihood of the BI file becoming full and causing a system stoppage.

2.   The IO display is a histogram indicating the percentage contribution of each Oracle process to the total amount of logical and physical Input/Output. Each process is identified by a Process Identification (PID). This can alert the database administrator to those processes that appear to be consuming an excessive amount of I/O.

3.   The Locks display indicates the condition of all the locks that are present in the system. For each process, it shows those locks that it has placed on various data objects in the system, and those locks that it is awaiting to be released. This can sometimes be useful in tracing the source of a perceived deterioration in system performance. It can reveal the situation when many processes are waiting on the release of a data object that is currently locked up by another process. This can happen, for instance, when a number of users are attempting to perform a SQL*Plus Update command on the same table. The first user to access the table will implicitly place a lock on it that prevents other users from Updateing it until the first user logs off or issues Rollback or Commit commands.

4.   The Summary screen displays the following system wide information:

     (a)   Log reads: the number of logical blocks read from the blocks found in the cache buffer pool in the SGA
     (b)   Phy reads: the number of physical disk blocks read
     (c)   Log writes: the number of modifications to cache buffer blocks
     (d)   Phy writes: the number of physical blocks written
     (e)   DML commits: the number of data manipulation commits
     (f)   DML rollbacks: the number of data manipulation rollbacks
     (g)   DDL commits: the number of data definition commits
     (h)   DML rollbacks: the number of data definition rollbacks
     (i)   Deadlocks: the number of system-wide deadlocks detected.

The same information can be displayed for single processes or sets of processes by use of the user command. This displays additional information such as the number of timeouts a process has been posted while awaiting the release of a resource, and the current operation being performed by a process. As well as information about user processes, the user command can be used to display information about the background processes. For instance, monitoring the CLN process indicates how successful this process is in its function of flushing the SGA of unused data objects.

5.   Finally, the Table display indicates the names and users of each table currently listed in the tables cache in the SGA.

Detailed analysis of the information derived from the display screens may lead the DBA to certain conclusions about the system performance. By adjusting certain of the parameters in the Init.Ora file, system performance can be enhanced.

For instance, the amount of data that can be put into main memory for fast access and processing can be increased by raising the level of the Buffers, Columns, Tables and Tablenames parameters. This causes more space to be assigned in SGA to these items. However, this also has the effect of increasing the size of the SGA. In virtual memory operating systems, performance will degrade if the SGA is continually being swapped in and out of memory, which becomes increasingly likely to happen as it gets bigger.

Various other parameters such as Table_Accesses, Table_Handles, Enqueues, Open-Cursors, Processes, Transactions and Users are *capacity parameters*. That is, they can be increased to raise the level of system performance without affecting the SGA size. However, they should be altered with care. For instance, raising the Processes parameter which limits the number of processes that can be activated at any one time without correspondingly raising the Table_Accesses and Enqueues parameters will almost certainly cause system bottlenecks. This is because an increased number of allowable processes will require a greater number of tables to be accessed, which will, in turn, necessitate a greater number of locking queues to be allowed. Failure to set parameters at correspondingly appropriate levels can cause operational problems.

8.5   Re-sizing and adding database files

As a database is in use, its files will gradually fill up. Ideally the database administrator will anticipate the database files becoming full before it happens, otherwise the users will one day receive this message:

Out Of Space In Partition

This tells the user that the physical files assigned to the partition in which they are working are full. When this happens, the DBA should shut down and back-up the database and add a new file to the partition.

To do this, a file has first to be created at the operating system level. This is done using the CCF (Create Contiguous File) utility. The syntax for CCF is:

CCF filename size

The filename should follow the conventions laid down by the operating system, and the size is a number indicating the number of operating system blocks to be allocated to this file. Thus, to create a file called MoreData of 5000 blocks in length, the command would be:

CCF 'MoreData' 5000

This file must now be added to the relevant partition. To do this, the database should be warm started in DBA mode. The database administrator can now log on to the system through a DBA account and issue the following SQL*Plus command:

Alter Partition System Add File 'MoreData'

where System is the name of the partition that is being increased in size. The name of a different partition should be substituted for System if it is a different partition that has been effected. The database may now be shut-down and re-started in full user mode. Only accounts with DBA status can alter partitions in this way. DBA accounts can also create new partitions. The command:

Create Partition Part1

will create a new partition with the name Part1. Before it can be used, it must have one or more files assigned to it, following the routine described above.

A DBA can monitor the condition of partitions by use of the SQL*Plus command:

SELECT SPMPID, SPMENDBLOCK − SPM$STARTBLOCK + 1
FROM SYS.SPACEMAP;

typically giving a display such as:

SPM$PID	SPM$ENDBLOCK − SPM$STARTBLOCK + 1
1	2342
1	87
1	456
1	45

In this output, SPM$PID indicates the number of the partition (1 being System) and each row indicates the amount of free space available in each unused contiguous block in a partition. The partition full error occurs either when a table is created for the first time or when an extent is being added to it. For either of these operations to succeed, there must be at least one contiguous block available with enough space in it to satisfy the space demand made by the table creation or extension.

A partition with a large number of small blocks is said to be in a *fragmented* condition. This will result in wastage of disk space as there will be a certain amount of space that cannot be assigned to tables because it is in blocks that are too small to satisfy any table requests. Fragmentation can be reduced by selectively dropping user tables or by performing a full database export/import. This is because when the tables are exported, they are compressed into contiguous blocks, thus combining all free space in a partition into a single block.

As mentioned above (Chapter 2, Section 3), each time a table is created in an Oracle database, a default space is assigned to it by the system. The typical default space defintion is:

```
Create Space Definition Default
     DataPages  (Initial 5
                 Increment 25
                 MaxExtents 9999,
                 PctFree 20)
     IndexPages(Initial 5,
                 Increment 25,
                 MaxExtents 9999)
     Partition System;
```

The basic syntax of a space definition is governed by the fact that a stored table consists of data and indexes over that data. The space assigned for an index may be as great, or even greater than, the space assigned for the data over which it is built. This allows the creation of multiple indexes over a single table.

The definition above first of all determines the space to be assigned to the data segment of a table. The Initial parameter tells the system to set aside 5 blocks of storage for data. The size of a block is operating system dependent, but is typically 2 or 4 kilobytes. The Increment parameter denotes how many extra blocks to assign when the initial allocation is full. MaxExtents indicates the number of times an additional allocation may be made. PctFree indicates what percentage of the logical block size should be reserved for updates to the data.

The same parameters are used, apart from PctFree, when specifying an index segment. The Partition clause specifies in which partition this space definition is available.

The Database Administrator will frequently wish to use the

Create Space Definition command to add extra space definitions to the data dictionary and instruct the users to specify them when creating tables. Judicious use of the appropriate space definitions when creating tables will reduce the amount of fragmentation in a database partition. Typically, in the commercial situation, the default space allocated to a file is far too small. By creating and using a much larger space definition, the file will take an appropriately sized portion of its resident partition in the first instance instead of constantly 'nibbling away' at the available free space, leaving the partition in a highly fragmented state.

A space definition is assigned to a table using the following version of the Create Table syntax:

```
Create Table TableName
     (   ***Attribute Definitions***   )
     Space Space_Definition_Name;
```

As well as checking for the existence of the space definition designated, Oracle software will also check which partition the space definition has been allocated to and assign the table to that partition. In this way, tables can be assigned to partitions other than the System partition, albeit indirectly.

As well as the database files, the Before Image file can become full. Once again, ideally the database administrator will have anticipated this (by use of the ODS facility), but it can happen while the database is live and cause an operating error.

To re-size the BI file, the database should be shut-down and the BI file backed up. If it has been shut down in Clear mode, it must be immediately brought up in DBA mode and shut down again in Shut mode in order to roll back any partially completed transactions with the old BI file. The CCF utility can now be used to create a new, larger BI file, taking care to use the name given to it in the Init.Ora file. The database may now be re-started in full user mode.

8.6 Summary

This chapter has necessarily given a brief overview of some of the facilities provided by Oracle to enable efficient management of a multi-user database. Like the best referees, a good database administrator will often appear to outsiders not to be doing very much. This is because, due to their managerial and technical skills, the system never seems to need attention. However, database administration is a very challenging and time-consuming task, and one not to be undertaken lightly. In addition to a technical mastery of the system, the database administrator must also be a master politician, balancing and attempting to satisfy the (often conflicting) requirements of the user community. Although

Oracle provides tools that help with the technical management of a system, the author is not aware that they or any other vendor supply tools that aid the political management!

Key points

- A multi-user Oracle database requires a Database Administrator to control and manage the use of the database.

- Starting and stopping an Oracle database is performed using the IOR command. This command allocates (or de-allocates) the SGA (System Global Area) in the main memory and starts up (or closes down) the detached processes that govern the operation of the database.

- Enrolling and dropping the users of an Oracle database is done using SQL commands available to an account with DBA privileges.

- The EXP, IMP and AIJ utilities are available for backing up and restoring an Oracle database.

- The ODS (Oracle Display System) provides a Database Administrator with the facility to monitor the live use of an Oracle database.

- Extra disk space can be added to an Oracle database by use of the Alter Partition and CCF commands.

- Only DBA accounts have the ability to create or alter partitions.

EXERCISES

8.1 Explain how the System Global Area and the background processes interact to service the reading and writing requirements of an Oracle user process.

8.2 In what ways can a Database Administrator ensure the integrity and security of an Oracle database?

8.3 What information does the ODS system provide to the Database Administrator? What uses can be made of this information?

Reference

The ORACLE Database Administrator's Guide, Oracle Part No. 3601-V5.1

Nine
Some Example Oracle Applications

In this chapter the creation of some simple database applications using Oracle will be discussed. The examples we will look at are:

- A library database of books and authors
- An airline reservations system
- A student administration system.

For each application, a set of tables representing the data content of the system will be created and forms for using the system will be designed. For the student administration system, some SQL*Plus programs will also be written.

The set of tables created for each application represents the optimal storage stucture for that application, that is the replication of non-key data across different tables is eliminated. The tables have been arrived at using the usual techniques of data normalization. A full discussion of normalization and data analysis is outside the scope of this book, and the reader who is interested in this important topic or who proposes to design a production database application will need to read a standard text such as Date (1986) or Pratt & Adamski (1987).

159

9.1   A library database of books and authors

The Manfield University Library contains a number of books arranged into coded categories according to the Dewey decimal system. Each book has a title, at least one author, a unique ISBN (International Standard Book Number), and a publisher with an address. For convenience, books are only recorded as belonging to one category. Each author is assigned a number in order to differentiate those authors with the same name. There may be more than one copy of a book in the library. Every physical copy of every book in the library is given a unique accession number. The database can be modelled with the following tables:

> Books: *ISBN* Title PubName DeweyCode
> Copies: *AccessionNo* ISBN
> Authors: *AuthorNo* Name
> Categories: *DeweyCode* Name
> Writers: *ISBN AuthorNo*
> Publishers: *PubName* Address

The primary key of each table has been printed in *italic* type.

The Books table contains the basic information for each book. PubName acts as a foreign key into Publishers in order to find the address of a book's publisher, while DeweyCode acts as a foreign key into Categories to yield its category. The Copies table contains a row for every copy of every book in the library, with the ISBN acting as a foreign key into Books. For each author there is a row in the Authors table. The Writers table establishes the relationship between a book and its contributing authors, with a row entered for every book that an author has contributed to. The authors are identified by the foreign key AuthorNo and the books that they have written are identified by the foreign key ISBN.

In setting up the library database, two user accounts will be created: Librarian and Reader. The Librarian account will own all the tables in the database and thus have full update and access rights, the Reader account will have access rights only to the tables.

The first thing that must be done is to log in to Oracle via a DBA account and issue the following two commands:

> GRANT CONNECT,RESOURCE TO LIBRARIAN IDENTIFIED BY password;
> GRANT CONNECT TO READER IDENTIFIED BY READER;

Notice how the Reader account has been given Connect rights only. That way, they can only browse through information in the database, they cannot add or alter any information at all with this account. The password is transparent as anyone should be able to access this account.

We now log in to the Librarian account to create the above described tables thus:

```
Create Table Books
      (ISBN Char (20) Not Null,
      Title Char (50),
      PubName Char (30),
      DeweyCode Number );

Create Table Publishers
      (PubName Char (30) Not Null,
      Address Char (50) );

Create Table Authors
      (AuthorNo Number Not Null,
      AuthorName Char (20) );

Create Table Categories
      (DeweyCode Number Not Null,
      Name Char (20) Not Null );

Create Table Copies
      (AccessionNo Number Not Null,
      ISBN Char (20) );

Create Table Writers
      (AuthorNo Number Not Null,
      ISBN Char (20) Not Null );
```

For each table, the primary key attribute (or set of attributes) has been specified as one which is not allowed to take null values. This restriction could have been on other attributes as well. For instance, it would probably be sensible to insist that every book has a title, so the Title attribute in Books could have been specified as Not Null. These sort of decisions need to be taken in consultation with the database user (in this instance, the Chief Librarian).

In order to ensure the uniqueness of the primary key attributes, unique indexes must be built over them:

```
Create Unique Index BookISBN
On Books (ISBN);

Create Unique Index PublisherName
On Publishers (PubName);

Create Unique Index AuthorsNo
On Authors (AuthorNo);

Create Unique Index CategoryCode
On Categories (DeweyCode);

Create Unique Index AccessionNo
On Copies (AccessionNo);
```

```
Create Unique Index AuthorBook
On Writers (AuthorNo, ISBN);
```

It would also be useful to create some secondary indexes. For example, it can be anticipated that the Books table will probably be queried according to a book's title. There will also probably be a lot of queries based on books that belong to the same category. Thus, the following indexes could be created to speed up these sorts of queries:

```
Create Index BooksName
On Books (Title);
```

```
Create Index ClassCode
On Books (DeweyCode);
```

Having got as far as setting our tables and indexes, they can now be made accessible to other users, though we may wish to do this after some data has been entered into them. To grant the Reader account access to these tables, the following commands must be given:

```
Grant Select On Books To Reader;
```

```
Grant Select On Publishers To Reader;
```

```
Grant Select On Authors To Reader;
```

```
Grant Select On Copies To Reader;
```

```
Grant Select On Writers To Reader;
```

```
Grant Select On Categories To Reader;
```

A number of forms can be built now to allow the Librarian to update the database and for the Librarian and the Reader to browse through the database.

9.1.1   Creating forms for the library database

Four forms will be created for the Librarian to update the database: one for entering the initial details of a book, one for updating the Dewey catalogue descriptions, one for updating the accessions list and one for updating publisher details.

The form for entering the initial details of a book will be composed of three blocks built over the Books, Authors and Writers tables respectively. The default form definition will be as shown in Figure 9.1.

The reader will be aware that many books have more than one author. In its present form, the Librarian would need to fill in each block in turn in order to update the underlying tables. To speed this up, it would be useful for the ISBN value in the Books block to be automatically entered into the Writers block when the cursor is moved there. This can be achieved by modifying the field definition for ISBN in the Writers block via the Validation window accessed from the Define

```
                  ======== BOOKS ========
         ISBN _____
        TITLE _____
    PUBLISHER _____ DEWEYCODE _____

                 ======== AUTHORS ========
    AUTHORNO      AUTHORNAME
    _____    _____
    _____    _____
    _____    _____

                 ======== WRITERS ========
    AUTHORNO      ISBN
    _____    _____
    _____    _____
    _____    _____


  Char Mode: Replace         Page: 1           Count: *0
```

Figure 9.1   Default form for initial entry of book details.

Field window. It can be specified here that the value for ISBN must be copied from the ISBN value in the Books block. The window for this is shown in Figure 9.2. It would also be useful for the catalogue specification to be displayed next to the Dewey number so the Librarian can see that the book is correctly classified. This can be done by creating a new field (ClassName) in the Books block following the procedure described in Chapter 5 and writing the following Post-Change trigger on the DeweyCode field:

```
Select Name
Into Classname
From Categories
Where Categories.DeweyCode =:Books.DeweyCode
```

Finally, the Screen Painter should be used for entering appropriate instructions onto the form. The eventual appearance may be something like that shown in Figure 9.3. The user is reminded of the option in the Authors block to query the database for those authors already listed. This is because any attempt to insert authors that already exist would raise an error due to the unique index on AuthorNo in the Authors table. Thus, the Authors block is used for inserting new authors and discovering the numbers of existing authors, whereas the Writers block

```
======== BOOKS ========
+-----------------------------------+
|           DEFINE FIELD    Seq # 2 __ |
| Name ISBN _____       |
|  +-------------------------------+-+
|  |      SPECIFY VALIDATION         |          _____
|  | Field Length 20 __  Query Length 20 __ |   DEWEYCODE _____
|  | Copy Field Value from:          |
|  |      Block BOOKS _____   |   ========
|  |      Field ISBN _____   |
+--| Default    _____    |
|  | Range Low_____        |
|  |     High _____        |
|  | List of Values:                 |
|  |     Table _____       |
|  |     Column _____      |   ========
|  | Help:                           |
AU| Enter value for :   ISBN _____|
 --+-------------------------------+-+
```

Form: BOOKDETAIL   **Block:** Writers   **Page:** 1   **SELECT:** 1   **Char Mode:** Replace

Figure 9.2   Amending the Field Definition for WRITERS ISBN.

Form for Initial Entry of Book Details

            ISBN _____
           TITLE _____
      PUBLISHER _____ DEWEYCODE _____

For each author new to the library, enter their author number and name. The database may be queried for authors already in the library.

AUTHORNO   AUTHORNAME

_____   _____
_____   _____
_____   _____

Enter below the number of each author contributing to the book above. The ISBN will be automatically entered to establish the author/book connection.

AUTHORNO   ISBN

_____   _____
_____   _____
_____   _____

Char Mode: Replace   **Page:** 1   **Count:** *0

Figure 9.3   Amended appearance of form for entry of book details.

is used for establishing the link between a book and its authors, who may or may not be on the database when the book is first entered.

The Librarian forms for creating and updating the Dewey catalogue descriptions and the publisher details are simple one-block forms built over Categories and Publishers respectively and are created quite easily. Figure 9.4(a) and (b) illustrate what the default options should give for these forms. The Categories form can be created as a multi-row display enabling many categories to be listed at once. Publishers can only be a single-row block as it has fields that are more than 20 characters wide.

With the accessions list, it would be useful to have two blocks: one built over the Copies table in order to update this table and one built over the Books block in order that this table may be queried to find out the ISBN for different books. A two-block form with appropriate headings may look something like the one shown in Figure 9.5. In the Books block, the <cut> and <paste> functions of the screen painter can be used to remove the publisher's name and the Deweycode from the display. This could be done if it was decided that the Librarian only wanted this block here in order to find the ISBN that relates to a particular book title, or vice versa.

As the Librarian account has ownership of these tables, each of these forms can be used to add to, delete from or amend the relevant records, subject to the constraints imposed by the Not Null and Unique Index specifications created over certain of their attributes. Forms created from the Reader account will only have the ability to browse through these tables as the Reader account has been granted Select powers only.

The base tables for the readers' forms will all contain the pre-fix Librarian. indicating that they are being built over tables belonging to the Librarian account. Thus, Books becomes Librarian.Books, Copies becomes Librarian.Copies and so on. For the Reader account, two forms will be created: one for searching the catalogue according to book details; and one for searching it according to author details. This author/book division of a library catalogue is quite common. Also, if desired, a default form over Categories would be created for those readers who are not *au fait* with the Dewey system.

The Book form will be a two-block from built over Books and Writers, laid out as suggested in Figure 9.6.

In this form, the Screen Painter has been used to write instructions to the user onto the form and to create an extra field (Authorname) in the Writers block. The two blocks can be tied together by using the Validation window for the ISBN field in Writers to force it to display duplicate values only of the ISBN field in the Books block. Also, a Post-change trigger needs to be written on Authorno in order to

```
========= CATEGORIES =========

DEWEYCODE        NAME
_____  _____
_____  _____
_____  _____
_____  _____
_____  _____
_____  _____
_____  _____
_____  _____
_____  _____
_____  _____




Char Mode: Replace           Page: 1            Count: *0
```

(a)

```
========= PUBLISHERS =========

     NAME _____

     ADDRESS _____






Char Mode: Replace           Page: 1            Count: *0
```

(b) *Figure 9.4* Default Forms for CATEGORIES and PUBLISHERS tables (a) Updating the Dewey catalogue. (b) Updating Publisher details.

retrieve the matching Authorname from the Authors table thus:

```
Select AuthorName
Into Writers.AuthorName
From Librarian.Authors
Where Librarian.Authors.AuthorNo = :Writers.AuthorNo
```

Having set up the screen thus, the <enter query> key on the Books block must be re-defined so that the Writers block is queried simultaneously. This can be done by means of the following block-level trigger on Key-Entqry for the Books block:

```
#EXEMACRO   NXTBLK; CLRBLK; PRVBLK; ENTQRY;
            NXTBLK; EXEQRY; PRVBLK;
```

Taken in order, these commands will:

1. Jump from the Books block to the Writers block (NXTBLK);
2. Clear the Writers block (CLRBLK);
3. Jump back to the Books block (PRVBLK);
4. Await the user to enter the search criteria (ENTQRY);
5. Jump to the Writers block (NXTBLK) causing the ISBN in Books to be replicated in the lower block;
6. Execute a query in this block based on this replicated ISBN (EXEQRY);
7. Return to the Books block (PRVBLK).

Some queries in the Books block will cause a set of books to be retrieved. As the operator scans this set of books retrieved by use of the <next record> key, the authors in the lower block should also be amended so that they continue to be matched against the book displayed in the higher block. This can be achieved with the following block-level trigger on KEY-NEXTREC in the Books block:

```
#EXEMACRO   NXTBLK; CLRBLK; PRVBLK; NXTREC;
            NXTBLK; EXEQRY; PRVBLK;
```

These function calls collectively will:

1. Jump to the Writers block and clear it (NXTBLK; CLRBLK);
2. Return to the Books block and retrieve the next record (PRVBLK; NXTREC);
3. Jump back to the Writers block causing the new ISBN to be copied across (NXTBLK);
4. Execute a query based on this ISBN (EXEQRY) and return to the Books block (PRVBLK).

```
=======  COPIES  =======


For each copy of a book, enter its accession number and ISBN code

ACCNO      ISBN

_____   _____

_____   _____

_____   _____

_____   _____

_____   _____


=======  BOOKS =======
Book details may be queried below:
Press <enter query> key,
Enter ISBN code of book:    _____
or
Enter title of book:        _____
and press <execute query> key.
```

| **Char mode:** Replace | **Page:** 1 | **Count:** *0 |

Figure 9.5   Form for entering copies of a book into the library.

```
=======  BOOKS =======
To find the details of a book or set of books:
press <enter query> and fill in as many details as you can below;
then press <execute query>.

        ISBN _____
        TITLE _____
   PUBLISHER _____
   DEWEYCODE _____


=======  WRITERS =======
Details of authors will be automatically displayed below.

ISBN              AUTHORNO          AUTHORNAME

_____   _____   _____

_____   _____   _____

_____   _____   _____
```

| **Char Mode:** Replace | **Page:** 1 | **Count:** *0 |

Figure 9.6   Form for querying library according to book details.

```
┌──────────────────────────────────────────────────────────────────┐
│                                                                    │
│              ======== AUTHORS ========                             │
│                                                                    │
│     1 Press <enter query>                                          │
│     2 Enter name of author _____    │
│     3 Press <execute query>                                        │
│     4 Details of any books that author has written will be displayed│
│       below.                                                       │
│                                                                    │
│     AUTHORNO        ISBN            BOOKTITLE                       │
│     _____    _____      _____              │
│     _____    _____      _____              │
│     _____    _____      _____              │
│     _____    _____      _____              │
│     _____    _____      _____              │
│     _____    _____      _____              │
│     _____    _____      _____              │
│     _____    _____      _____              │
│     _____    _____      _____              │
│                                                                    │
│   ────────────────────────────────────────────────────────────    │
│   Char Mode: Replace            Page: 1            Count: *O       │
└──────────────────────────────────────────────────────────────────┘
```

Figure 9.7   Form for querying catalogue via Author's Details.

This form is specifically set up to enable the catalogue to be queried via book details, with author details being retrieved automatically, without user intervention. It is similar in concept to the form discussed in Chapter 5 in its master/servant relationship between the two blocks. The form for querying the catalogue according to author details will have this sort of relationship again between the two blocks, only this time, Authors will be the master block, with Books taking the subservient role.

This second query form will, again, have two blocks, the first created over the Authors block, the second over the Writers block. The appearance of this form will be as indicated in Figure 9.7.

To create this form the author's block has been implemented as a single row block and the <cut> and <paste> functions were used to visually separate the AuthorNo from the AuthorName. The AuthorName heading has been replaced by an explanatory message, as has the heading for the Writers block.

On the Writers block, a column has been incorporated for the title of each book that the queried author has contributed to. As this is a column that does not come from the base table over which the block has been created, it can be inserted on the same line as the other columns without worrying about its actual width being more than 20 characters.

Its display width is just as it is drawn; this way, the block can retain its multi-row characteristic. For books with titles longer than the width displayed, the <left scroll> and <right scroll> keys can be used to read the entire title.

As with the previous form, the two forms need to be tied together with a Validation attribute, defined, this time, on the AuthorNo in the Writers block, to ensure it always has the same value as the AuthorNo in the Authors block. A Post-change trigger on ISBN in the Writers block will have to be written to retrieve all book titles belonging to this author thus:

```
Select Title
Into Writers.Title
From Librarian.Books
Where Librarian.Books.ISBN = :Writers.ISBN
```

The querying of the two blocks can be tied together by re-defining the <enter query> and <next record> keys in exactly the same way as it was for the books query form.

On each of these two query forms, data such as ISBN and AuthorNo are visually replicated across the blocks. It is possible to blank out the display of these fields on the forms by switching off the Display attribute for a field from the Specify Attributes window accessed via the Define Field window in the Screen Painter. This renders a field invisible on a form, but does not invalidate any references made to it through triggers and so on.

9.2 An airline reservation system

The Fly-By-Night Chartered Airline Company arranges flights to all parts of the world from Buxton. Each flight has a unique flight number, a time of departure, a day of the week on which it flies out and a destination. To make a reservation on a flight, the passenger has to supply their name and address. They are then allocated a seat number; they are also allocated a class, which determines the fare that is payable for a particular flight.

The system may be modelled by the following tables:

Flights: FlightNo Time Day Destination

Reservations: FlightNo SeatNo Name Address Class

Fares: FlightNo Class Fare

For each reservation, a composite primary key consisting of the FlightNo and the SeatNo must be specified. FlightNo in this instance is, of course, a foreign key into Flights. Fares also has a composite key consisting of FlightNo (to reference the flight) and Class (to identify the class of fare for that flight).

To operate the system, two accounts have been set up, a Controller account with the full set of privileges (Connect, Resource and DBA) and an Operator account which has Connect privilege only. The Controller defines and owns the underlying tables and forms whereas Operator uses them to enter and alter reservation data. The tables listed above are set up in the Controller account thus:

```
Create Table Flights
(FlightNo Char(10) Not Null,
Time Num(4),
Day Char(3),
Destination Char(10) );

Create Table Reservations
(FlightNo Char(10) Not Null,
SeatNo Number Not Null,
Name Char (20),
Address Char (60),
Class Char(1) );

Create Table Fares
(FlightNo Char(10) Not Null,
Class Char (1) Not Null,
Fare Number (8,2) );
```

Having created the tables, indexes can now be built over the keyfield attributes for each table:

```
Create Unique Index FlNo On Flights (FlightNo);
Create Unique Index Resx On Reservations
(FlightNo, SeatNo);
Create Unique Index Farex On Fares (FlightNo, Class);
```

Since it is likely that the Flights table will frequently be queried according to the destination of a flight, it will be useful to create an index over the Destination attribute:

```
Create Index Dest On Flights (Destination);
```

The Operator account should have the ability to update the Reservations data. This account should also be able to access Flight and Fare details, but it should not be able to alter the data in these tables. Thus, the following privileges will be given to the Operator account:

> Grant Select, Insert, Update, Delete On Reservations
> To Operator;
> Grant Select On Fares To Operator;
> Grant Select On Flights To Operator;

Having set up the base tables and privileges, some forms can now be created for the system.

9.2.1   Forms for the airline reservation system

Two forms need to be created: one for the Controller account to set up flight details and fares, and one for the Operator account to enter and alter reservation details.

The Controller's form is shown in Figure 9.8. It is built over two blocks: Flight and Fares, built over the Flights and Fares tables respectively. Each is built in a straightforward manner using the default options with no extra fields added. Flight is a single record block, whereas Fares is a multi-record block, as there can be more than one fare per flight.

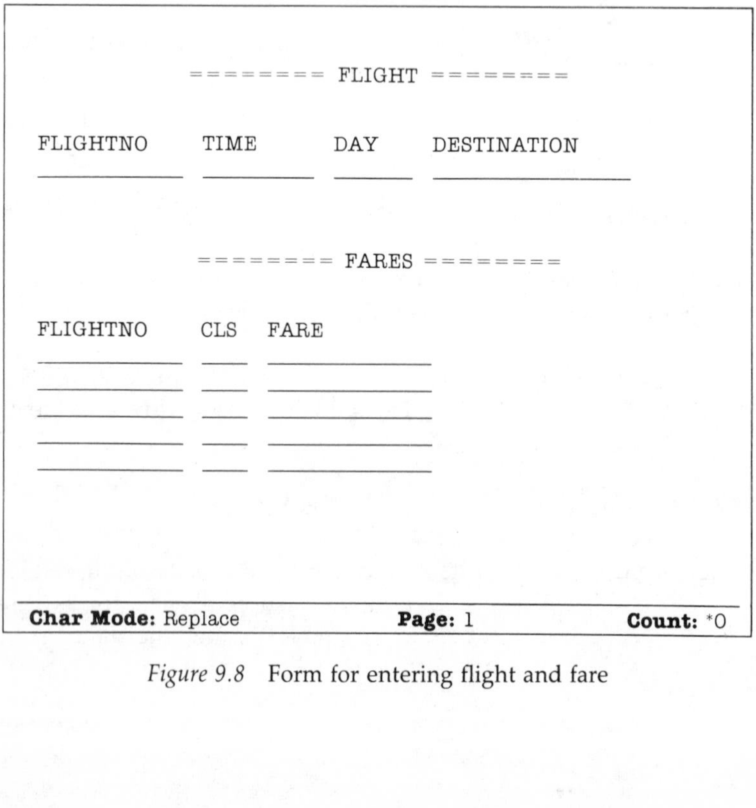

Figure 9.8   Form for entering flight and fare

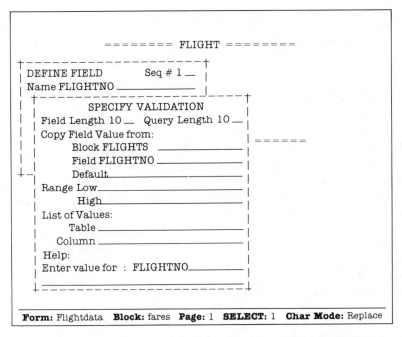

```
              ======== FLIGHT ========

+-----------------------------+
| DEFINE FIELD        Seq # 1 __ |
| Name FLIGHTNO _____    |
|    +-----------------------------+
|    |        SPECIFY VALIDATION        |
|    | Field Length 10 __  Query Length 10 __ |
|    | Copy Field Value from:            |    ======
|    |     Block FLIGHTS  _____  |
|    |     Field FLIGHTNO _____  |
+ -  |     Default _____  |
|    | Range Low _____  |
|    |      High _____  |
|    | List of Values:                  |
|    |     Table _____  |
|    |     Column _____  |
|    | Help:                            |
|    | Enter value for : FLIGHTNO _____ |
|    +-----------------------------+
+-----------------------------+
```

Form: Flightdata **Block:** fares **Page:** 1 **SELECT:** 1 **Char Mode:** Replace

Figure 9.9 Amending the definition of FLIGHTNO in the FARES block.

The form is modified in order that a query entered on the Flight block will display the Fares for a given Flight. This is done in three stages:

1. Specify a validation attribute on FlightNo in the Fares block that causes it to copy its value from the FlightNo value in the Flight block. This is shown in Figure 9.9.

2. Write a block-level trigger on the <enter query> key (KEY-ENTQRY) in the Flight block that causes the system to jump to the Fares block, clear it, return to the Flight block to enter the query parameters and then to execute a query based on the copied Flightno in the Fares block:

    #EXEMACRO NXTBLK; CLRBLK; PRVBLK; ENTQRY; NXTBLK; EXEQRY; PRVBLK;

3. Write a block-level trigger in the Flights block to ensure that, as the user moves from one record to another in this block, the fares information for each Flight record is displayed in the Fares block. As with the Library system, this is achieved by writing a Trigger

on the <next record> key (KEY-NXTREC):

#EXEMACRO NXTBLK; CLRBLK; PRVBLK; NXTREC;
NXTBLK; EXEQRY; PRVBLK;

Having constructed the Controller's form, the Operator's form for entering reservation details can now be created – see Figure 9.10.

This is also a two-block form, built over Flights and Reservations. The Screen Painter has been used to customize the headings slightly. Both blocks are single-record blocks, the top block deliberately so. Ideally, the lower block would be a multi-record block reflecting a series of reservations for a flight, but, as the Reservations table is more than 80 characters wide, it is not possible to display more than one complete record at a time on the screen.

The two blocks can be tied together in the same manner as the operator's form to ensure that queries performed on the Flights block result in the reservations for that flight appearing in the Reservations block.

The Reservations block has an extra field, Fare, added to display the fare for a reservation. This is determined by the class of the reservation and is recorded in the Fares table. This means that the following Post-change trigger has to be written on the Class field in the

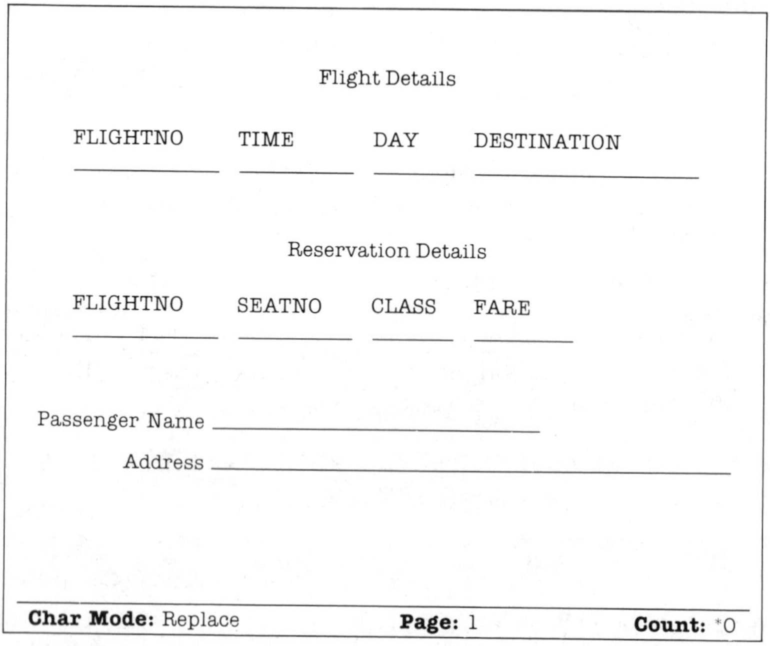

Figure 9.10 Operator's form for entering reservation details.

```
                          Flight Details
    +------------------------------------+
    |         DEFINE BLOCK      Seq # 2 _ | DESTINATION
    | Name    RESERVATIONS _____ | _____
    +------------------------------------+-----------------+
    | SPECIFY DEFAULT ORDERING                             |
    | WHERE / ORDER BY clause for QUERY                    |
    | ORDER BY SEATNO _____|
    | _____ |
    | _____ |
    | _____ |
    | _____ |
    | Actions:  FORWARD   BACKWARD   DELETE                |
    +------------------------------------------------------+
             Address _____

  ----------------------------------------------------------------
  Form: BOOKINGS   Block: DETAILS   Page: 1   SELECT: B   Char Mode: Replace
```

Figure 9.11   Using the SPECIFY DEFAULT ORDERING window.

Reservations block:

> Select Fare Into Fare
> From Fares
> Where Fares.Class = :Reservations.Class
> And Fares.FlightNo = :Reservations.FlightNo

This trigger will cause the Fares table to be examined to find the fare that relates to the flight number and class specified on the Reservations block.

It would be preferable when querying the Reservations block for the records to be retrieved in seat number order for a particular flight. This can be done by <select>ing the action Ordering from the Define Block window which brings up the Specify Default Ordering window. This enables the form designer to specify the order in which records should be displayed in a block by entering an appropriate SQL Order By clause. Thus, entering the phrase Order By SeatNo in this window will cause all records retrieved by a query to be displayed in seat number order. This window is shown in Figure 9.11.

The reader may notice that a Where clause may also be entered in this window. This enables the records to be displayed in a block to be subject to some sort of user-defined global restriction. Where and Order By may be used in the same clause, subject to the SQL syntax rules.

9.3   A student administration system

Crammers' College run a number of courses on a modular basis. Each course consists of a number of units, all of which are chosen from a list of options. Each unit is identified by a course number and a unit number. A student may enrol on to any number of courses and on to any of the units within a course. A separate enrolment is recorded for each course. The set of courses and units that a student is following is known as their program of study. The system is modelled by the following tables:

```
Courses: CourseNo CourseName CourseLeader
Students: StudNo Name Address
Enrolments: StudNo CourseNo EnrolDate
Units: CourseNo UnitNo UnitName Tutor
Programs: StudNo CourseNo UnitNo Mark
```

The Enrolments table represents the relationship between a student and the set of courses they are enrolled on to. As a student may only enrol on to a course once, the StudNo/CourseNo combinations for each row has to be unique, and are thus sufficient to act as the primary key for this table. The same applies to the Programs table which represents the relationship between a student's enrolment on to a course and the set of units that they study. Here, the StudNo/CourseNo/ UnitNo combinations are unique, as a student cannot logically be enrolled onto a unit of a course more than once. The composite key Unitno/Courseno for Units is necessary as the same Unitno may occur in different courses. An alternative scheme would be necessary if Units formed part of more than one course. In this case, *all* Unitnos would have to be unique, Courseno would have to be removed from the Units table, and an extra table CourseUnits would have to be formed comprised of the columns Courseno and Unitno representing the relationship between a course and the units that contribute to it.

These tables and the necessary indexes can be created in a straightforward manner.

```
Create Table Courses
(CourseNo Char(10) Not Null,
CourseName Char(30)
Leader Char(20) );
Create Unique Index CrsNo On Courses (CourseNo);
```

```
Create Table Students
(StudNo Number Not Null,
Name Char(20);
Address Char(80) );
Create Unique Index SNo On Students (StudNo);

Create Table Enrolments
(StudNo Number Not Null,
CourseNo Char(10) Not Null,
EnrolDate Date );
Create Unique Index End On Enrolments (StudNo, CourseNo);

Create Table Units
(CourseNo Char 10) Not Null,
UnitNo Char (5) Not Null,
UnitName Char(40),
Tutor Char(20) );
Create Unique Index UNo On Units (CourseNo, UnitNo);

Create Table Programs
(StudNo Number Not Null,
CourseNo Char(10) Not Null,
UnitNo Char(5) Not Null,
Mark Number);
Create Unique Index On Programs (StudNo, CourseNo, UnitNo);
```

9.3.1   Forms for the student administration system

Two forms will be constructed for the system: one for entering and altering the details of a course and its constituent units, a second for entering and altering a student's details and their program of study.

The course details form shown in Figure 9.12 comprises two blocks: Courses built over the Courses table and Units built over the Units table.

The two blocks on this form can be tied together by specifying a validation on Courseno in the Units block to force it to take its value from the Courseno in the Courses block and then to write block-level triggers in the Courses block re-defining the <enter query> and <next record> keys to cause the Units block to be simultaneously queried on the CourseNo value copied from Courses. These triggers are exactly the same as those described in Sections 9.1.1 and 9.2.1.

The Student Details form (Figure 9.13) is slightly more complex in that it comprises three blocks:

1.   Student, built over the Students table;

2.   Enrolment, built over the Enrolments table; and

3.   Program, built over the Programs table.

```
         ======== COURSE ========

COURSENO _____   COURSENAME _____

         ======== UNIT ========

COURSENO   UNITNO   UNITNAME              TUTOR
_____   _____   _____   _____
_____   _____   _____   _____
_____   _____   _____   _____
_____   _____   _____   _____
_____   _____   _____   _____
_____   _____   _____   _____
_____   _____   _____   _____
_____   _____   _____   _____
_____   _____   _____   _____
_____   _____   _____   _____
_____   _____   _____   _____
```

Char Mode: Replace   **Page:** 1   **Count:** *0

Figure 9.12   The Course Details Form.

```
         ======== STUDENT ========

   STUDNO _____   NAME _____
  ADDRESS _____

         ======== ENROLMENT ========

STUDNO   COURSENO   COURSENAME      ENROLDATE
_____   _____   _____   _____

         ======== PROGRAM ========

STUDNO   COURSENO   UNITNO   UNITNAME
_____   _____   _____   _____
_____   _____   _____   _____
_____   _____   _____   _____
_____   _____   _____   _____
_____   _____   _____   _____
_____   _____   _____   _____
_____   _____   _____   _____
_____   _____   _____   _____
_____   _____   _____   _____
```

Char Mode: Replace   **Page:** 1   **Count:** *0

Figure 9.13   The Student Details form.

On this form, the blocks must be tied together so that the records displayed in the Enrolment and Program blocks relate to the Student record in the Student block. The processes are, in fact, basically the same as those performed on previous forms.

Firstly, two validations are specified: one on the Enrolment block StudentNo to force it to take a duplicate of the StudentNo in the StudentNo and one in the Program block to force it to copy its value from the Enrolment block StudentNo. This way, the same StudentNo is replicated across the form as the cursor moves from one block to the next. A validation must also be specified on CourseNo in the Program block to force it to copy its value from CourseNo in the Enrolment block. This way, the set of units displayed in the Program block relate to the course displayed in the Enrolment block.

Secondly, triggers have to be written on the <enter query> and <next record> keys in the Students block to enable the data displayed in the other blocks to be related to queries executed in this top block. These triggers will be similar to the ones written in previous sections, except that they require two blocks to be cleared and queried instead of one, thus entailing extra commands. The trigger on KEY-ENTQRY will be:

```
#EXEMACRO   NXTBLK; CLRBLK; NXTBLK; CLRBLK;
            PRVBLK; PRVBLK;
            ENTQRY; NXTBLK; EXEQRY; NXTBLK;
            EXEQRY;
            PRVBLK; PRVBLK;
```

The Trigger on KEY-NXTREC will be similarly extended:

```
#EXEMACRO   NXTBLK; CLRBLK; NXTBLK; CLRBLK;
            PRVBLK; PRVBLK;
            NXTREC; NXTBLK; EXEQRY; NXTBLK;
            EXEQRY;
            PRVBLK; PRVBLK;
```

On the Enrolment block, the shorter versions of these Triggers are needed to enable the program of study displayed in the bottom block to be tied to queries on the Enrolment block. This is useful for situations such as finding programs of study for all students on a given course, or finding the different programs of study for a given student.

9.3.2 SQL*Plus programs for the student administrative system

A common requirement for any educational database is the ability to produce lists.

Crammers College need a comprehensive list of all their classes to be produced at the end of the enrolments period. This is achieved with the program below which generates lists of students grouped according to their courses and within the units on each course, thus giving a comprehensive register for every unit on every course.

```
Spool Master_Student_List
Set NewPage 6
Set Page 54
Break On CourseNo Skip Page On CourseName
        On UnitNo Skip Page On UnitName On Tutor
Compute Count Of Name On UnitNo
Compute Count Of Name On CourseNo

Select Programs.CourseNo, CourseName, Programs.UnitNo,
        UnitName, Tutor, Name
From Students, Units, Programs, Courses
Where Students.StudNo = Programs.Studno
    And Programs.UnitNo = Units.UnitNo
    And Programs.CourseNo = Courses.CourseNo
    And Programs.CourseNo = Units.CourseNo
  Order By Programs.CourseNo, Programs.UnitNo, Name ;

Clear Breaks
Clear Computes
Spool Out
```

The SQL*Plus commands at the start of the program set up a pagesize that will leave a one-inch margin above and below the top of each page of a report printed on paper 11 inches long. The Break commands prevent the Course and Unit heading information from being unnecessarily repeated across every record retrieved from the database. They also enable a count to be performed on the number of students in each unit and on each course. The Skip commands enable each unit listing to be displayed on a new page.

The SQL Select command performs the joins required to derive the course/unit listing from the database, with the Order By part ensuring that the output is grouped as required.

There will be frequent occasions when a single unit listing rather than a global listing is required. A command to produce a listing of any unit register is as follows:

```
Select Unitname, Tutor, Name
from Units, Programs, Students
where Units.UnitNo = &UnitNo
    and Programs.CourseNo = &CourseNo
    and Programs.UnitNo = Units.UnitNo
    and Units.CourseNo = Programs.CourseNo
    and Students.Studno = Programs.Studno
order by Name;
```

This command prompts the operator to enter a UnitNo value and a CourseNo value and then generates a unit list according to these parameters. The Order By clause is simpler, as the output no longer has to be in Course/Unit order.

9.4   Summary

In this chapter, some prototype databases for maintaining a series of simple systems have been put together very quickly. Although only a subset of the facilities available in SQL*Plus and SQL*Forms has been used, it provides the basis for a set of usable systems. The reader may have noticed, for instance, that no provision has been made for any borrowers of books from the library as yet. This can be tackled quite simply by creating two new tables: Borrower, containing a row for every person that the library lends books to and Borrows, containing a row for every book currently on loan consisting of foreign keys into Borrower and Copies respectively to establish the relationship between a borrower and the set of books that they borrow. Appropriate forms can then be built over the resulting tables.

This speed and flexibility of application development comes as a result of Oracle's success in adding 'Fourth Generation' computing tools to a relationally complete DBMS. It is hard to imagine how long, complicated and error-ridden a process it would be to build similar systems using more traditional data processing methodologies and languages.

EXERCISES

9.1   Crammers College have decided to install the Manfield University library system. They wish to extend the system to include borrowers.

Assuming that a student may borrow a set of books design a Borrowers form built over two blocks. The top block will be built over the Students table. The lower block will be built over a new table consisting of a row for every book currently on loan to a student. The table will comprise two attributes: the StudentNo of the Student and the AccessionNo of the book. This block will be displayed with additional fields indicating the title of each book on loan and the main author. The overall layout of the form will be as below:

====== STUDENT ======

StudentNo	StudentName

Address

	Books On Loan
StudentNo	AccessionNo

Title

Main Author

Triggers will need to be written to retrieve the book information from the tables in the library database and the form customized so that a query executed on the Students block will retrieve the set of books on loan to a student in the lower block.

9.2 The Fly-by-Night airline company requires a report indicating the total amount of revenue generated per flight. Write the SQL*Plus command file necessary to generate the following report from the database:

Flightno	Destination	No. of Passengers	Value of Fares

Write extra commands indicating the average revenue generated per flight, and the average fare paid by each passenger on each flight.

References

Pratt P.J. and Adamski J.J. (1987) *Database Systems: Management and Design*: Boyd & Fraser.

C.J. Date (1986). *An Introduction to Database Systems* Vol. 1. Reading, MA: Addison-Wesley.

PART THREE
Appendices

Appendix A
SQL Commands Summary

In the syntax descriptions given in the Appendices, the following conventions are observed :

- CAPITALS indicate words that are a required part of a clause.

- [ ] indicates those parts of a clause that are optional.

- { } indicates those parts of a clause or sub-clause that are compulsory.

- | is used in those clauses or sub-clauses where there is a choice of allowable words and/or sub-clauses.

- UNDERLINED CAPITALS indicate a required word that Oracle defaults to and automatically assumes to be present unless an alternative is specified.

- . . . at the end of a sub-clause indicates that it may be repeated.

For simplicity, the syntax descriptions given overleaf summarize only that which has been discussed in the text. Complete syntax descriptions of all Oracle commands may be found in the relevant Oracle manuals.

A.1   Data manipulation and retrieval

A.1.1   The SELECT command

SELECT [ALL | DISTINCT]
{ * | expression [,expression ...] }
FROM table [alias] [,table [alias] ...]
[WHERE condition]
[GROUP BY expression [,expression ...]
[HAVING condition]
[{UNION | INTERSECT | MINUS} SELECT-command]
[ORDER BY {column-reference | integer} [ASC | DESC]
    [,{column-reference | integer} [ASC | DESC] ...] ;

An expression may be a column-reference, a function call (AVG, MAX, MIN, STDDEV, SUM, VARIANCE), an arithmetic expression involving column-references and/or function-calls or a literal.

A column-reference may specify the table from which the column comes and the owner of the table. This is required when column names are ambiguous. A column reference may alternatively include a tuple variable which must be specified as an alias next to the table name.

A condition takes the following form:

[NOT] { expression { = | != | > | | <= | >= }
    { expression | (SELECT-command) } |
  expression [NOT] BETWEEN expression AND
  expression |
  column-reference [NOT] LIKE comparative-item |
  column-reference IS [NOT] NULL |
  expression [NOT] IN { comparative-item | (SELECT-
  command) } |
  EXISTS (SELECT-command) }
[AND | OR { condition } ...]

A.1.2   The INSERT command

INSERT INTO table [column [,column ...]]
{ VALUES (value [,value ...]) | SELECT-statement } ;

A.1.3   The DELETE command

DELETE FROM table [WHERE condition] ;

A.1.4   The UPDATE command

UPDATE table [alias]
    { SET column = expression [,column = expression ...] |
    SET (column [,column ...]) = (SELECT-command) }
    [WHERE condition] ;

A.2 Data definition

```
CREATE TABLE table
 (column-specification [NOT NULL]
  [,column-specification [NOT NULL]... ] )
 [SPACE space-name]
 [AS SELECT-statement] ;

CREATE VIEW viewname [alias [,alias ... ]]
AS SELECT-command ;

CREATE [UNIQUE] INDEX indexname
ON table (column [ASC | DESC] [,column [ASC | DESC] ... ]);

CREATE PARTITION partition-name;
(For DBA use only)

CREATE SPACE [DEFINITION] space-name
[DATAPAGES(
     [INITIAL { 5 | integer}]
     [INCREMENT {25 | integer}]
     [MAXEXTENTS {9999 | integer}]
     )]
[INDEXPAGES(
     [INITIAL { 5 | integer}]
     [INCREMENT {25 | integer}]
     [MAXEXTENTS {9999 | integer}]
     )][PARTITION {SYSTEM | partition-name}] ;

ALTER PARTITION partition-name ADD FILE filename ;
(For DBA use only)

ALTER SPACE [DEFINITION] space-name
[DATAPAGES(
     [INITIAL { 5 | integer}]
     [INCREMENT {25 | integer}]
     [MAXEXTENTS {9999 | integer}]
     )]
[INDEXPAGES(
     [INITIAL { 5 | integer}]
     [INCREMENT {25 | integer}]
     [MAXEXTENTS {9999 | integer}]
     )]
[PARTITION {SYSTEM | partition-name}] ;

ALTER TABLE table
{ ADD | MODIFY }
 (column-specification [NOT NULL]
  [,column-specification [NOT NULL]... ] ) ;

DROP { TABLE table | VIEW viewname | INDEX indexname |
       SPACE [DEFINITION] space-name } ;
```

A.3   Access control

GRANT [CONNECT,] [RESOURCE,] [DBA,] TO user [,user ...]
[IDENTIFIED BY password [,password ...]] ;
(For DBA use only)

GRANT { ALTER | DELETE | INDEX | INSERT | SELECT | UPDATE |
     ALL }
ON table TO { user [,user ...] | PUBLIC } ;

REVOKE [CONNECT,] [RESOURCE,] [DBA] FROM user [,user ...]
(For DBA use only)

REVOKE { ALTER | DELETE | INDEX | INSERT | SELECT | UPDATE |
     ALL }
ON table FROM { user [,user ...] | PUBLIC } ;

Appendix B
SQL*Plus Commands Syntax

The syntax of those SQL*Plus commands discussed in the text only are described here. A full listing of all SQL*Plus commands will be found in the Oracle SQL*Plus Reference Manual.

B.1   Report formatting commands

```
BRE[AK] { ON { expression | ROW | PAG[E] | REPORT } ... }
         [SKI[P] integer | [SKI[P]] PAGE]
         [NODUP[LICATES] | DUP[LICATES]] ;
BRE[AK] ; (* displays all current BREAK values*)
COMP[UTE] [AVG | COU[NT] | MAX[IMUM] | MIN[IMUM] |
          NUM[BER] | STD | SUM | VAR[IANCE] ... ]
     OF { expression | label [,expression | label ... ] }
     ON { expression | label | PAGE | REPORT | ROW }
COMP[UTE] (* displays all current computes *)
COL[UMN] { column | expression }
          [FOR[MAT] format-specification]
          [HEA[DING] text
          [JUS[TIFY] { LEFT | CENTRE | RIGHT } ]]
          [LIKE { expression | label }]
          [ON | OFF]
COL[UMN] (* displays all current column specifications *)
CL[EAR] { BREAK | COLUMNS | COMPUTES } ;
BTI[TLE] [COL[UMN] integer]
          [SKIP [1 | integer]
          [TAB integer]
          [LEFT | RIGHT | CENTER]
          [FORMAT character]
          [character | variable] ...
```

BTI[TLE] (* displays current page footer title *)

BTI[TLE] { OFF | ON }

TTI[TLE] [COL[UMN] integer]
        [SKIP [1 | integer]
        [TAB integer]
        [LEFT | RIGHT | CENTER]
        [FORMAT character]
        [character | variable] ...

TTI[TLE] (*displays current page header title *)

TTI[TLE] { ON | OFF }

B.2   User environment commands

SET [BUFFER buffername]
    [HEA[DING] { OFF | ON }]
    [LINE[SIZE] {80 | integer }]
    [PAGES[IZE] {14 | integer }]
    [PAU[SE] { OFF | ON | text }]
    [SQLP[ROMPT] { SQL› | text }]
    [SQLN[UMBER] { ON | OFF }]
    [SQLT[ERMINATOR] { ; | character | ON | OFF }]
    [SUFFIX { sql | text }] ;

There are, in all, 42 system variables that can be controlled using the SET command. Those given here are the ones referred to in the text.

DESCRIBE table ;

HELP [command | help-topic] ;

ROLL[BACK] ;

COMMIT;

NEWPAGE [1 | integer] ;

PAUSE text ;

REMARK text;

B.3   Command editing and management

A[PPEND] text

C[HANGE] /oldtext/newtext

I[NPUT] text

DEL (*deletes last line of current buffer*)

EDIT filename

L[IST] [integer] (*displays SQL buffer*)

SAV[E] filename

START filename

GET filename

RUN (*executes contents of SQL buffer*)

Appendix C
SQL*Forms Windows Summary

In this appendix, each window will be described in terms of its usage, fill-ins and keys. Some windows also contain switches that select/de-deselect a given attribute. For these windows, just the usage and the switches are described.

Since on most of the windows, most of the actions result in another window being instantiated, a diagram with each window that summarizes the effects of each action. These diagrams together comprise a navigation guide through the SQL*Forms windows.

An action is designated by the use of capital letters, for example, RUN, whereas a key-stroke is designated by the use of [ ] e.g. [accept] indicating the key that causes the [accept] function.

This appendix is not exhaustive. Only those windows referred to in the text are described. Furthermore, those windows which simply list a series of objects to be selected (e.g. List Forms, List Blocks, List Columns etc.) are not included.

C.1   The Choose Form window

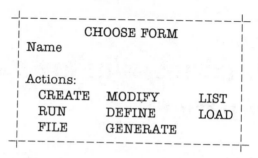

Figure C.1(a)   The Choose Form window.

- *Usage*: Selecting a form to work with.
- *Fill-Ins*:
  – Name   Name of the form.
- *Keys*:
  – [accept]   Exit from SQL*Forms.
  – [select]   Select action marked by cursor.

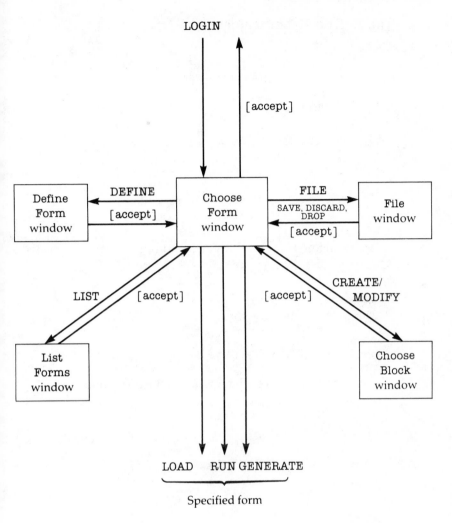

Figure C.1(b)   The effects of each action in the Choose Form window.

C.2   The Define Form window

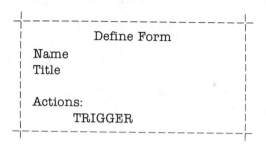

Figure C.2(a)   The Define Form window.

- *Usage*: To define form-level triggers and other properties of the form.
- *Fill-Ins*:
  - Name: Name of form.
  - Title: Descriptive title for form.
- *Keys*:
  - [accept]:   Preserve changes and return to Choose Form window.
  - [exit/cancel]:   Cancel changes and return to Choose Form window.
  - [select]:   Select action marked by cursor.

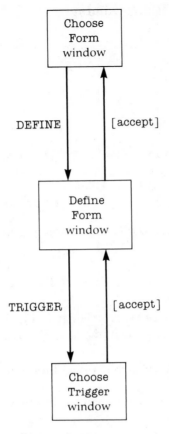

Figure C.2(b) The effects of each action in the Define Form window.

C.3 The Choose Block **window**

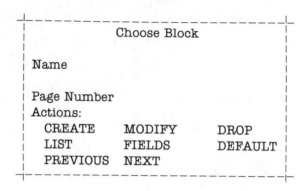

```
+-------------------------------------------+
|                Choose Block               |
|                                           |
| Name                                      |
|                                           |
| Page Number                               |
| Actions:                                  |
|    CREATE    MODIFY      DROP             |
|    LIST      FIELDS      DEFAULT          |
|    PREVIOUS  NEXT                         |
+-------------------------------------------+
```

Figure C.3(a)   The Choose Block window.

● *Usage*: Select a block to create, modify or drop.
● Fill-ins:
   – **Name**:   Name of block to create or modify.
   – **Page number**:   Page number to display.
● *Keys*:
   – [accept]:   Preserve changes and return to Choose form window.
   – [exit/cancel]:   Cancel changes and return to Choose form window.
   – [select]:   Select action marked by cursor.

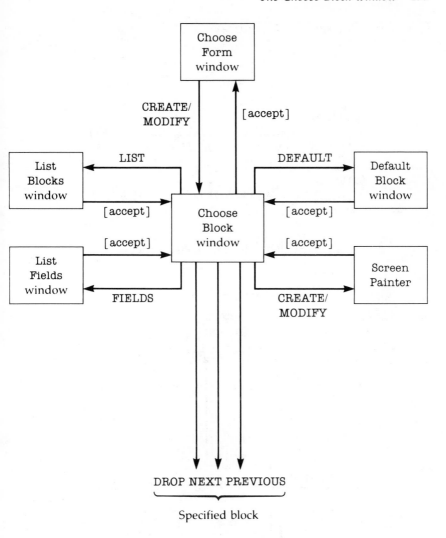

Figure C.3(b)   The effects of each action in the Choose Block window.

C.4   The Define Field window

```
_|_____|_
 |            Define Field              Seq#  |
 | Name:                                      |
 | Data Type:                                 |
 | *CHAR     NUMBER    RNUMBER    DATE         |
 |   ALPHA   INT       RINT       JDATE        |
 |   TIME    MONEY     RMONEY     EDATE        |
 | Actions:                                   |
 |   TRIGGER    ATTRIBUTES    VALIDATION       |
 |   COLUMNS                                   |
_|_____|_
```

Figure C.4(a)   The Define Field window.

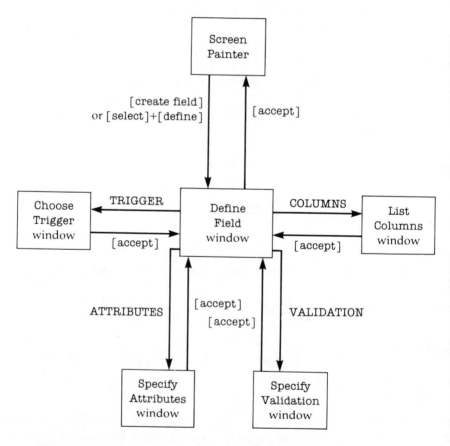

Figure C.4(b)   The effects of each action in the Define Field window.

- *Usage*: Define the properties of a field.
- *Fill-ins*:
  - Seq#:   Order in which cursor moved to this field.
  - Name: Name of associated column in base table (database fields). Any other valid name for non-database fields.
- *Switches*:
  - Data Type: Select one from the data types listed to determine data type and display format of field.
- *Keys*:
  - [accept]:   Preserve changes and return to screen painter.
  - [exit/cancel]:   Cancel changes and return to screen painter.
  - [select]:   Select action marked by cursor.

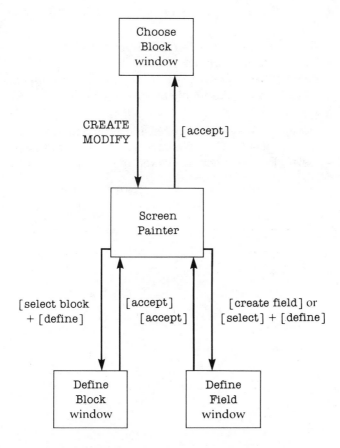

Figure C.4(c) The effects of each action in the Screen Painter window.

C.5 The Define Block window

```
 |----------------------------------------------L
 +----------------------------------------------+
 |              Define Block            Seq#     |
 | Name:                                         |
 | Description:                                  |
 | Table Name:                                   |
 | Actions:                                      |
 | TRIGGER   ORDERING OPTIONS    TABLES          |
 +----------------------------------------------L
```

Figure C.5(a)   The Define Block **window.**

- *Usage*:   Define properties of current block.
- *Fill-Ins*:
    - Seq#:   Order in which cursor moves to block.
    - Name: Name of block.
    - Description: Description to appear on block menu.
    - Table Name: Base table or view for block.
- *Keys*:
    - [accept]:   Preserve changes and return to screen painter.
    - [exit/cancel]:   Cancel changes and return to screen painter.
    - [select]:   Select action marked by cursor.

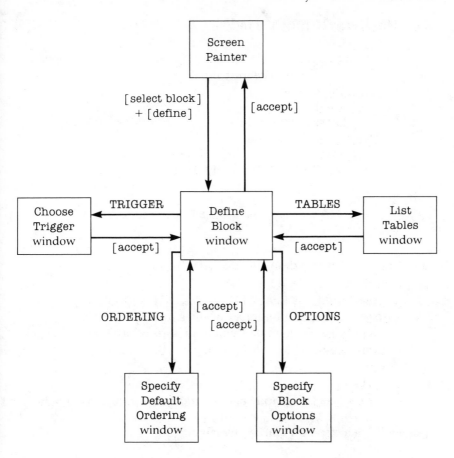

Figure C.5(b) The effects of each action in the Define Block window.

C.6   The Default Block window

```
+------------------------------------------------+
|                  Default Block                 |
| Table Name:                                    |
|                                                |
| Rows Displayed : 1                             |
|       Base Line : 1                            |
| Actions:                                       |
|      COLUMNS            TABLES                  |
+------------------------------------------------+
```

Figure C.6(a)   The Default Block window.

- *Usage*: Specify field layout of a default block.
- *Fill-ins*:
  - Table Name: Name of base table or view for block.
  - Rows Displayed: Number of rows displayed at one time.
  - Base Line: Screen line number on which block should begin.
- *Keys*:
  - [accept]:   Preserve changes and return to Choose Form window.
  - [exit/cancel]:   Cancel changes and return to Choose Form window.
 - [select]:   Select action marked by cursor.

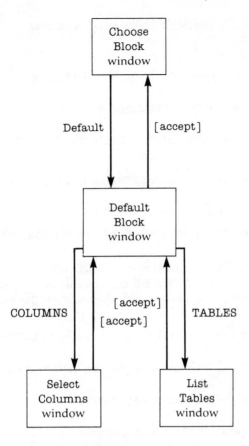

Figure C.6(b)   The effects of each action in the Default Block
window.

C.7   **The** Specify Default Ordering **window**

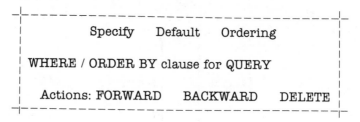

Figure C.7(a)   The Specify Default Ordering window.

- *Usage*:   To control the way records are retrieved into a block.
- *Fill-ins*:
  - **WHERE / ORDER BY** clause for **QUERY**:   Specifies **SQL**
    WHERE and/or **ORDER BY** clauses that are clause for
    incorporated into every query executed on the block.
- *Keys*:
  - [accept]:   Preserve changes and return to Define Block
    window.
  - [exit/cancel]:   Cancel changes and return to Define Block
    window.
  - [select]:   Select action marked by cursor.

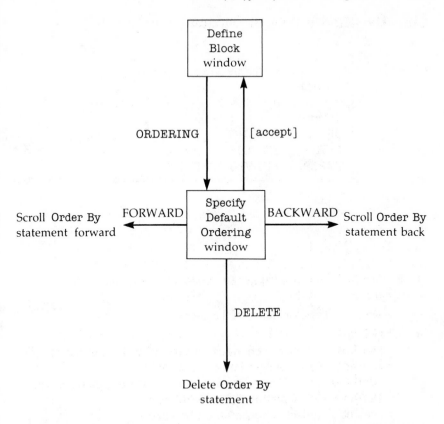

Figure C.7(b) The effects of each action in the Specify Default Ordering window.

C.8   **The** Choose Trigger **window**

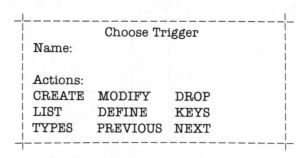

```
 |--------------------------------------|
 |              Choose Trigger          |
 | Name:                                |
 |                                      |
 |                                      |
 | Actions:                             |
 | CREATE    MODIFY     DROP            |
 | LIST      DEFINE     KEYS           |
 | TYPES     PREVIOUS   NEXT            |
 |--------------------------------------|
```

Figure C.8(a)   The Choose Trigger window.

- *Usage:*   To select a trigger to create or modify it.
- *Fill-ins:*
  – Name: Type or name of Trigger.
- *Keys:*
  – [accept]:   Preserve changes and return to Define Block, Define Field or Define Form window.
  – [exit/cancel]:   Cancel changes and return to Define Block, Define Field or Define Form window.
  – [select]:   Select action marked by cursor.

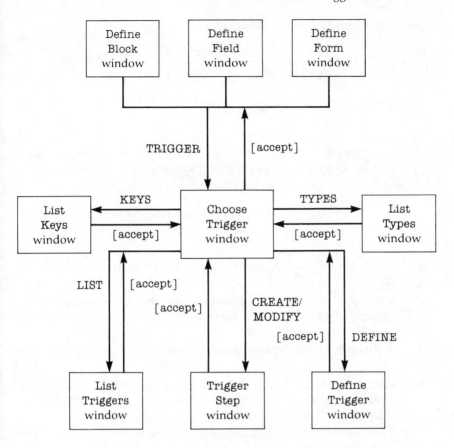

Figure C.8(b) The effects of each action in the Choose Trigger window.

C.9 The Trigger Step window

```
+----------------------------------------------------------+
|                                                          |
|  Seq # 1          Trigger Step        Label              |
|                                                          |
|  Message if trigger step fails:                          |
|                                                          |
|  Actions:                                                |
|        CREATE     COPY          DROP         ATTRIBUTES  |
|        FORWARD    BACKWARD   PREV STEP    NEXT STEP       |
+----------------------------------------------------------+
```

Figure C.9(a) The Choose Trigger Step window.

- *Usage*: Specifies a command to be executed in the current trigger.
- *Fill-ins*:
  - Seq #:   The order in which this step should be executed.
  - Label: Name by which this step can be branched to form another step.
  - Message if trigger step fails: Message to be displayed on failure of step.
- *Keys*:
  - [accept]:   Preserve changes and return to Choose Trigger window.
  - [exit/cancel]:   Cancel changes and return to Choose Trigger window.
  - [select]:   Select action marked by cursor.

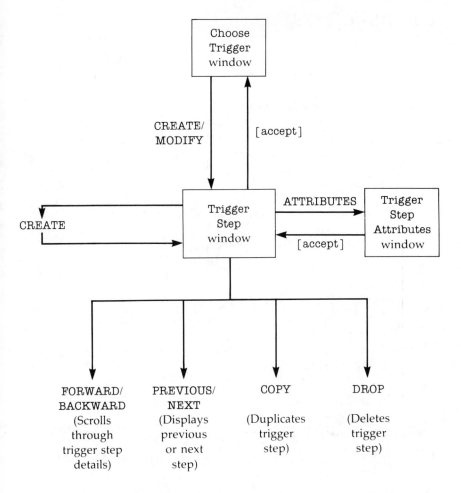

Figure C.9(b) The effects of each action in the Trigger Step window.

C.10   **The** Trigger Step Attributes **window**

```
+------------------------------------------------+
|           TRIGGER   STEP   ATTRIBUTES          |
|                                                |
|        *Abort trigger when step fails          |
|         Reverse return code                    |
|         Return success when aborting trigger   |
|         Separate cursor data area              |
|                                                |
|  Success label                                 |
|  Failure label                                 |
+------------------------------------------------+
```

Figure C.10   The Trigger Step Attributes window.

- *Usage*: To specify what happens when trigger step succeeds or fails.
- *Switches*:
  - Abort trigger when step fails: Halts execution of trigger if step fails. Over-ridden if failure label is entered.
  - Reverse return code: Reverses criteria for success and failure of trigger.
  - Return success when aborting trigger: Causes trigger to succeed if it is being aborted due to failure of current step.
  - Separate cursor data area: Reserves memory space for trigger step.
- *Fill-ins*:
  - Success/Failure label: Specifies next step to be executed.

C.11   The Specify Attributes **window**

```
 _|_ _ _ _ _ _ _ _ _ _ _ _ _|_
|                            |
|  Specify Attributes        |
|                            |
|    *Database Field         |
|     Primary Key            |
|                            |
|    *Displayed              |
|    *Input Allowed          |
|    *Query Allowed          |
|    *Update Allowed         |
|     Update if NULL         |
|     Fixed Length           |
|     Mandatory              |
|     Uppercase              |
|     Autoskip               |
|     Automatic Help         |
|     No echo                |
|                            |
 _|_ _ _ _ _ _ _ _ _ _ _ _ _|_
```

Figure C.11   The Specify Attributes window.

- *Usage*:   To specify the characteristics of the current field.
- *Switches*:
  - Database Field: Field drawn from base table for block.
  - Primary Key: Field is part of record's unique key.
  - Displayed: Field is visible on form.
  - Input Allowed: Field values may be entered onto form.
  - Query Allowed: Query condition may be entered on field.
  - Update Allowed: Field values may be changed.
  - Update if NULL: Only NULL values may be changed.
  - Fixed Length: Field values must be exactly the length of the displayed field.
  - Mandatory: May not contain NULL values.
  - Uppercase: All characters displayed in uppercase.
  - Autoskip: Cursor moves immediately to next field on completion of fill-in.
  - Automatic Help: Help message automatically displayed.
  - No Echo: Value of field displayed as blanks.

C.12   The Specify Validation **window**

```
-|-------------------------------|-
|            Specify Validation            |
| Field Length 20        Query Length 20  |
| Copy Field Value from:                  |
|    Block                                |
|    Field                                |
| Default                                 |
| Range Low                               |
|         High                            |
| List of Values:                         |
|    Table                                |
|    Column                               |
| Help:                                   |
| Enter value for   :   CUSTNAME          |
-|-------------------------------|-
```

Figure C.12   The Specify Validation window.

- • *Usage*:   To validate user input and specify help message.
- • *Fill-ins*:
  - – Field Length: Maximum number of characters that may be entered into a field.
  - – Query Length: Maximum number of characters entered for a query condition.
  - – Copy Field Value: Specify block and field from which the field value may be copied.
  - – Default Range: Default value for new records maximum and minimum values for field.
  - – List of Values: Table and column containing list of valid values for field.
  - – Help: Message to appear when operator presses [Help] key.

Appendix D
Oracle Products Summary

In addition to the software tools described in the text, there are a number of additional products supplied by Oracle for use with an Oracle database. The facilities provided by each are briefly summarized below.

D.1 SQL*Calc

This is a spreadsheet program that is functionally equivalent to a Lotus 1-2-3 spreadsheet.

As with the Lotus product, a spreadsheet is composed of 'cells' which may contain numbers, words or values calculated from formulae entered by the user. (Fig. D.1). In addition to the Lotus 1-2-3 range of functions, cell values on a SQL*Calc spreadsheet can also contain SQL commands to reference an Oracle database. Any valid SQL statement can be entered, thus allowing the full range of SELECT, INSERT, DELETE and UPDATE operations to be performed on the database via the spreadsheet.

Data retrieved from an Oracle database into a spreadsheet may then be re-formatted and processed according to the Lotus 1-2-3 commands and options. Data may also be written from the spreadsheet display into the database via an SQL statement. The SQL syntax is extended to allow reference to be made to values held in cell locations. For instance, the following command can be entered as a cell value:

Select Sname from Stock where Sprice › &A20

This will retrieve into this cell the names of all items whose price is greater than the value entered into cell A20 on the spreadsheet. Update, Delete and Insert operations may also be executed by making reference to cell values.

	A	B	C	D	E	F	G	H
1								
2			GreenGroceries					
3								
4			Price/Kg.	Kgs.	Cost			
5								
6		Potatoes	0.25	5	1.25			
7		Sprouts	0.45	2	0.9			
8		Brocolli	0.37	2	0.74			
9		Parsnips	0.33	1	0.33			
10		Turnips	0.11	3	0.33			
11		Carrots	0.32	3	0.96			
12								
13		Total Cost			2.21			
14								
15								
16								
17								
18								
19								
20								
21								
22								
23								
24								
25								
26								
27								
28								
29								
30								

SQL*Calc   Range   Copy   Layout   File   Print   Oracle   Key   Quit
Worksheet

Figure D.1   A typical spreadsheet layout.

D.2   SQL*Menu

This program allows the creation and execution of menu-driven applications over an Oracle database. Menus are composed of options which may be selected for execution by the user. Selection of an operation may trigger the following type of action:

- Invoke SQL*Plus
- Invoke SQL*Forms
- Execute an operating system command
- Execute an operating system command followed by a pause

- Invoke a sub-menu
- Execute a SQL*Menu macro.

Invoking SQL*Plus will result in a valid SQL*Plus command being executed. Invoking SQL*Forms will result in a form created in SQL*Forms being presented for user operation. The ability to invoke a sub-menu enables the building of 'menu trees' where an application consists of a number of interrelated menus and options.

SQL*Menu macros are commands that manipulate menus. There are thirty in all and include the following example functions:

- Return to previous menu
- Show Help
- Show list of function keys
- Move to next menu
- Return to main menu
- Leave SQL*Menu
- Clear field
- Define substitution parameter

and so on.

As with the SQL*Forms, SQL*Menu is used in two modes: creating menus and using menus. Menus may be customized to include tailored headings and messages and to accept search parameters from the user.

D.3   Easy*SQL

Easy*SQL provides a menu-driven interface to an Oracle database. The aim is to provide the non-programming user the functionality of SQL*Plus without having to learn the language. This is achieved by means of pop-up windows, fill-in forms and option menus. The main menu options of Easy*SQL are as follows:

- QUERY   (*build, store, recall and execute queries*)
- REPORT   (*format, store, recall and execute reports*)
- EDIT   (*build applications*)
- CREATE   (*create tables*)
- GRAPH   (*draw graphs derived from data in database*)
- EXTENDED   (*create views, modify table definitions, update and delete data*)
- ADMINISTRATION   (*backup and expand the database, transfer data*).

Selection of any of these options then takes the user into another window which may itself consist of a menu or set of fill-in items.

D.4 Networked Oracle

The Oracle software provides various tools that allow data to be shared between different machines.

- *SQL*Net*. This tool allows an Oracle user on one machine to access an Oracle database on another. Access to a remote database may be specified when logging into Oracle itself by tagging the name and network address of the database onto the user's password. Within SQL*Plus itself, the CONNECT and COPY commands are provided. CONNECT allows a user to log on to a remote database while COPY allows data to be transferred from one database to another.

- *SQL*Star*. This tool allows an Oracle database to be distributed across a number of machines. The aim is to achieve *location transparency*; that is, a user may execute a query that makes use of data stored on and collected together from a number of machines without being aware that this is a case. To the user, the database should appear as a single entity.

- *SQL*Connect*. This allows an Oracle user to access and process data held on a DB2 database.

D.5 CASE

CASE (Computer Aided Systems Engineering) currently has two parts: CASE*Dictionary and CASE*Designer. CASE*Dictionary has grown out of the SQL*Design Dictionary, a suite of programs aimed at the system developer.

CASE*Dictionary provides the analyst/designer with a dictionary system built on top of an Oracle database that stores and controls the information collected and derived during the development and implementation of a system. It consists of approximately 90 online application screens built in SQL*Forms. The screens aim to cover every part of the system life cycle and address the following areas:

- Application and System definition
- Function Hierarchy
- Entity-Relationship Diagram definition
- Dataflow Diagram definition
- Function definition

- Detailed data, dataflow and datastore definition
- Default database design
- Database size prediction
- Program/module definition
- Program Documentation
- Database and conventional file definition
- Retrofit of existing Oracle database definitions
- Impact analysis definition
- Re-definition and Re-documentation

CASE*Dictionary has been devised to support Oracle's own SQL* Development Method, but is compatible with other structured method- ologies (SSADM, Yourdon, James Martin Associates etc.). The CASE* Design software makes use of workstation technology to provide a number of high-level graphics tools interfaced to CASE*Dictionary to further automate the system development process.

Index